SCRIPTURES

FOR

LIVING

Anita T. Williams

Scriptures for Living

ISBN: 979-8-234-00242-6

Book Cover, Editing, and Formatting by:

Pieces of Me Publication Services (POM)

~pompservices@gmail.com

Dedicated to my beloved children, grandchildren, great-grandchildren, all future descendants, and to all who understand the power of speaking, living, and praying the Word of God.

Table of Contents

Thy word is a lamp unto my feet, and a light unto my path.
Psalm 119:105 KJV

The entrance of Your words gives light; It gives understanding to the simple.
Psalm 119:130 NKJV

This Book of the Law shall not depart from your mouth, but you shall meditate on it day and night, so that you may be careful to do according to all that is written in it. For then you will make your way prosperous, and then you will have good success.
Joshua 1:8 ESV

Thanksgiving and Praise For Who He Is

O Lord, our Lord, how majestic is Your Name in all the earth! How excellent, magnificent, wonderful-how great is Your Name! His Name is identified as wide, large, and POWERFUL! His reputation defines His name, and His Name defines His character, and His character defines His word. Yahweh, the proper name of the God of Israel, who has now become our Sovereign God. Holy and perfect in all His ways of supreme power and authority. When His Word is spoken, it is activated and does not return to Him void; it accomplishes fully what He sends it to do. So enter into His gates with thanksgiving and into His courts with praise and glorify His Holy Name!

Hebrews 12:28-29 NIV
Therefore, since we are receiving a kingdom that cannot be shaken, let us be thankful, and so worship God acceptably with reverence and awe, for our God is a consuming fire. [Akal Esh]

1 Chronicles 16:23-26 NIV
Sing to the Lord, all the earth; proclaim his salvation day after day. Declare his glory among the nations, his marvelous deeds among all peoples. For great is the Lord and most worthy of praise; He is to be feared above all gods. For all the gods of the nations are idols, but the Lord made the heavens. [Creator: Elohim]

Psalm 108:1 NLT
My heart is confident in you, O God; no wonder I can sing your praises with all my heart!

Psalm 107:1-2 NKJV
Oh, give thanks to the Lord, for He is good! For His mercy endures forever. Let the redeemed of the Lord say so, Whom He has redeemed from the hand of the enemy. [Redeemer: Ga'al]

Psalm 106:48 AMPC
Blessed (affectionately and gratefully praised) be the Lord, the God of Israel, from everlasting to everlasting! And let all

the people say, Amen! Praise the Lord! (Hallelujah!)

Psalm 106:1-2 TLB
Hallelujah! Thank you, Lord! How good you are! Your love for us continues on forever. Who can ever list the glorious miracles of God? Who can ever praise him half enough?

Psalm 103:20-22 NKJV
Bless the Lord, you His angels, who excel in strength, who do His word, Heeding the voice of His word. Bless the Lord, all you His hosts, You ministers of His, who do His pleasure. Bless the Lord, all His works, in all places of His dominion. Bless the Lord, O my soul! [Most High God: El Elyon]

Psalm 105:1 KJV
O give thanks unto the Lord; call upon his name: make known his deeds among the people.

Jeremiah 31:3 ESV
The Lord appeared to him from far away. I have loved you with an everlasting love; therefore, *I have continued my faithfulness to you.* [The Faithful God: Ha'El hanne'eman]

Psalm 103:8-10 KJV
The Lord is merciful and gracious, slow to anger, and plenteous in mercy. He will not always chide: neither will he keep his anger forever. He hath not dealt with us after our sins; nor rewarded us according to our iniquities. [The Merciful God: El Rachum]

Psalm 103:17-18 KJV
But the mercy of the Lord is from everlasting to everlasting upon them that fear Him, and *His righteousness unto children's children*; To such as keep his covenant, and to those that remember his commandments to do them. [The Lord our Righteousness: Jehovah-Tsidkenu]

Psalm 98:1-3 NLT
Sing a new song to the Lord, for He has done wonderful deeds. His right hand has won a mighty victory; His Holy arm has shown His saving power! The Lord has announced His victory and has revealed his righteousness to every nation! He has remembered His promise to love and be faithful to Israel. The ends of the earth have seen the victory of our God. [The Lord My Banner: Jehovah Nissi]

Psalm 92:1-4 NLT
It is good to give thanks to the Lord, to sing praises to the Most High. It is good to proclaim your unfailing love in the morning, your Faithfulness in the evening. Accompanied by a ten-stringed instrument, a harp, and the melody of a lyre. You thrill me, Lord, with all you have done for me! I sing for joy because of what you have done.

Psalm 92:8 KJV
But thou, Lord, art most high for evermore.

Ephesians 1:19-20 NKJV
And what is the exceeding greatness of His power toward us who believe, according to *the working of His mighty power* which He worked in Christ when He raised Him from the dead and seated Him at His right hand in the heavenly places. [Lord God Almighty: El Shaddai]

Psalm 75:1 NKJV
We give praise and thanks to You, O God, we praise and give thanks; Your wondrous works declare that Your Name is near, and they who invoke Your Name rehearse Your wonders.

Ephesians 3:20 NKJV
Now to Him who is able to do exceedingly abundantly above all that we ask or think, according to the power that works in us.

Psalm 73:28 KJV
But it is good for me to draw near to God: I have put my trust in the Lord God, that I may declare all thy works.

Psalm 33:1 KJV
Rejoice in the Lord, O ye righteous: for praise is comely for the upright.

Jesus Christ, the Power of the Living Word in Us

In the beginning was the Word, and the Word was with God, and the Word was God. He was in the beginning with God. All things were made through Him, and without Him nothing was made, that was made (John 1:1-3 NKJV)—Jesus Christ, the Living Word of God in us. We are God's workmanship, which we were created in Christ for good works. "Exousia," the power of authority we have been given due to our positional standing in Christ Jesus. We have now been raised and seated in the heavenly places in Christ Jesus, far above all principalities, powers, etc. "Dunamis," the power, the force, and ability to be more than conquerors in any situation or circumstances through Christ Jesus.

Romans 1:16 KJV
For I am not ashamed of the gospel of Christ: for it is the power of God unto salvation to every one that believeth; to the Jew first, and also to the Greek.

2 Corinthians 12:9 ESV
And He has said to me, "My grace is sufficient for you, for power is perfected in weakness." Most gladly, therefore, I will rather boast about my weaknesses, so that the power of Christ may dwell in me.

1 Corinthians 1:18 KJV
For the preaching of the cross is to them that perish foolishness; but unto us which are saved it is the power of God.

1 Peter 1:3-5 NKJV
Blessed be the God and Father of our Lord Jesus Christ, who, according to His abundant mercy, has begotten us again to a living hope through the resurrection of Jesus Christ from the dead, to an inheritance incorruptible and undefiled and that does not fade away, reserved in heaven for you, who are kept by the power of God through faith for salvation ready to be revealed in the last time.

Philippians 4:13 NKJV
I can do all things through Christ who strengthens me.

1 Corinthians 1:24 ESV
But to those who are the called, both Jews and Greeks, Christ is the power of God and the wisdom of God.

Colossians 1:13 ESV
For He rescued us from the domain of darkness, and transferred us to the kingdom of His beloved Son.

John 5:25-26 ESV
Truly, truly, I say to you, an hour is coming and now is, when the dead will hear the voice of the Son of God, and those who hear will live. For as the Father has life in himself, so he has granted the Son also to have life in himself.

2 Peter 1:2-4 NKJV
Grace and peace be multiplied to you in the knowledge of God and of Jesus our Lord, as His divine power has given to us all things

that pertain to life and godliness, through the knowledge of Him who called us by glory and virtue. By which have been given to us exceedingly great and precious promises, that through these you may be partakers of the divine nature, having escaped the corruption that is in the world through lust.

Ephesians 2:6 AMP
And He raised us up together with Him and made us sit down together [giving us joint seating with Him] in the heavenly sphere [by virtue of our being] in Christ Jesus (the Messiah, the Anointed One).

Ephesians 1:16-23 NKJV
Do not cease to give thanks for you, making mention of you in my prayers: that the God of our Lord Jesus Christ, the Father of glory, may give to you the spirit of wisdom and revelation in the knowledge of Him, the eyes of your understanding being enlightened; that you may know what is the hope of His calling, what are the riches of the glory of His inheritance

in the saints, and what is the exceeding greatness of His power toward us who believe, according to the working of His mighty power. Which He worked in Christ when He raised Him from the dead and seated Him at His right hand in the heavenly places, far above all principality and power and might and dominion, and every name that is named, not only in this age but also in that which is to come. And He put all things under His feet, and gave Him to be head over all things to the church, which is His body, the fullness of Him who fills all in all.

Ephesians 3:20-21 AMP
Now to Him Who, by (in consequence of) the [action of His] power that is at work within us, is able to [carry out His purpose and] do superabundantly, far over and above all that we [dare] ask or think [infinitely beyond our highest prayers, desires, thoughts, hopes, or dreams]— To Him be glory in the church and in Christ Jesus throughout all generations, forever and ever. Amen (so be it).

1 Corinthians 12:27 AMP
Now you [collectively] are Christ's body and [individually] you are members of it, each part severally and distinct [each with his own place and function].

Acts 2:38 NKJV
Then Peter said to them, "Repent, and let every one of you be baptized in the name of Jesus Christ for the remission of sins; and you shall receive the gift of the Holy Spirit.

THE HOLY SPIRIT, OUR HELPER

The Holy Spirit, the Third Person of the God Trinity. He is also known as the Holy Ghost, the Spirit of God, the Spirit of Christ, the Spirit of Truth, and the Breath of God. He was asked for by the Son and sent by the Father to us. He came to help, comfort, guide, and teach, among many other things. We were sealed with the Holy Spirit of Promise, who is the Guarantee of our inheritance. He, who proceeds from the Father, is not only with you, but also in you to testify of Christ. He can be grieved, quenched, and sinned against, yet He can also be loved. He did not come to us empty-handed but brought gifts, so learn of Him and from Him.

Holy Spirit Guide Me! Help Me to Listen, Learn, and Remember

John 14:26 ESV
But the Helper, the Holy Spirit, whom the Father will send in my name, he will teach you all things and bring to your remembrance all that I have said to you.

Holy Spirit, Help Me to Pray

Romans 8:26 ESV
Likewise, the Spirit helps us in our weakness. For we do not know what to pray for as we ought, but the Spirit himself intercedes for us with groanings too deep for words.

Holy Spirit, help me walk, talk, and act right

Acts 1:8 NIV
But you will receive power when the Holy Spirit comes on you, and you will be my witnesses in Jerusalem, and in all Judea and Samaria, and to the ends of the earth.

John 3:8 NIV
The wind blows where it wishes, and you hear the sound of it, but do not know where it comes from and where it is going; so is everyone who is born of the Spirit.

Luke 11:13 NIV
If you then, being evil, know how to give good gifts to your children, how much more will your heavenly Father give the Holy Spirit to those who ask Him?

John 16:13-14 NKJV
However, when He, the Spirit of truth, has come, He will guide you into all truth; for He will not speak on His own authority, but whatever He hears He will speak; and He will tell you things to come. He will glorify Me, for He will take of what is Mine and declare it to you.

Help us, Holy Spirit

John 14:15-17 ESV
If you love me, you will keep my commandments. And I will ask the Father, and he will give you another Helper, to be with you forever. Even the Spirit of truth, whom the world cannot receive, because it neither sees him nor knows him. You know him, for he dwells with you and will be in

you.

2 Corinthians 3:17 ESV
Now the Lord is the Spirit, and where the Spirit of the Lord is, there is freedom.

Ephesians 6:18 ESV
Praying at all times in the Spirit, with all prayer and supplication. To that end, keep alert with all perseverance, making supplication for all the saints.

Zechariah 4:6 NIV
Not by might nor by power but by my Spirit, says the Lord God Almighty.

I Corinthians 2:12 NKJV
We have received, not the spirit of the world, but the Spirit who is from God, that we might know the things that have been freely given to us by God.

Fire is Illustrative of The Holy Spirit

Isaiah 4:4 NKJV
When the Lord has washed away the filth

of the daughters of Zion and purged the bloodshed of Jerusalem from her midst, by the spirit of judgment and the spirit of burning.

Acts 2:3 NKJV
And there appeared to them tongues as of fire distributing themselves, and they rested on each one of them.

Galatians 5:18 ESV
But if you are led by the Spirit, you are not under the law.

Romans 8:14 ESV
For all who are led by the Spirit of God are sons of God.

Galatians 5:19-26 AMPC
Now the doings (practices) of the flesh are clear (obvious): they are immorality, impurity, indecency, Idolatry, sorcery, enmity, strife, jealousy, anger (ill temper), selfishness, divisions (dissensions), party spirit (factions), sects with peculiar opinions, heresies, envy, drunkenness,

carousing, and the like. I warn you beforehand, just as I did previously, that those who do such things shall not inherit the kingdom of God. But the fruit of the [Holy] Spirit [the work which His presence within accomplishes] is love, joy (gladness), peace, patience (an even temper, forbearance), kindness, goodness (benevolence), faithfulness, Gentleness (meekness, humility), self-control (self-restraint, continence). Against such things there is no law [that can bring a charge]. And those who belong to Christ Jesus (the Messiah) have crucified the flesh (the godless human nature) with its passions and appetites and desires. If we live by the [Holy] Spirit, let us also walk by the Spirit. [If by the Holy Spirit we have our life in God, let us go forward walking in line, our conduct controlled by the Spirit.] Let us not become vainglorious and self-conceited, competitive and challenging, provoking and irritating to one another, envying and being jealous of one another.

Isaiah 11:2 ESV
And the Spirit of the Lord shall rest upon him, the Spirit of wisdom and understanding, the Spirit of counsel and might, the Spirit of knowledge, and the fear of the Lord.

Romans 15:30 AMP
I urge you, believers, by our Lord Jesus Christ and by the love of the Spirit, to join together with me in your prayers to God on my behalf.

Isaiah 63:10 NIV
Yet they rebelled and grieved His Holy Spirit. So he turned and became their enemy, and He himself fought against them.

Ephesians 4:30 KJV
And grieve not the Holy Spirit of God, whereby ye are sealed unto the day of redemption.

Genesis 1:2 ESV
The earth was without form and void, and darkness was over the face of the deep. And the Spirit of God was hovering over the face of the waters.

2 Peter 1:21 ESV
For no prophecy was ever produced by the will of man, but men spoke from God as they were carried along by the Holy Spirit.

Hebrews 9:14 ESV
How much more will the blood of Christ, who through the eternal Spirit offered himself without blemish to God, purify our conscience from dead works to serve the living God.

1 Corinthians 12:11 ESV
All these are empowered by one and the same Spirit, who apportions to each one individually as He wills.

Psalm 139:7 ESV
Where shall I go from your Spirit? Or where shall I flee from your presence?

Psalm 104:30 ESV
When you send forth your Spirit, they are created, and you renew the face of the ground.

Revelation 22:17 ESV
The Spirit and the Bride say, "Come." And let the one who hears say, "Come." And let the one who is thirsty come; let the one who desires take the water of life without price.

Hebrews 3:7-8 TLB
And since Christ is so much superior, the Holy Spirit warns us to listen to him, to be careful to hear his voice today and not let our hearts become set against him, as the people of Israel did. They steeled themselves against his love and complained against him in the desert while he was testing them.

1 Timothy 4:1-3 ESV
Now the Spirit expressly says that in later times some will depart from the faith by devoting themselves to deceitful spirits

and teachings of demons, through the insincerity of liars whose consciences are seared, who forbid marriage and require abstinence from foods that God created to be received with thanksgiving by those who believe and know the truth.

1 Thessalonians 1:5 KJV
For our gospel came not unto you in word only, but also in power, and in the Holy Ghost, and in much assurance; as ye know what manner of men we were among you for your sake.

Romans 8:11 NKJV
But if the Spirit of Him who raised Jesus from the dead dwells in you, He who raised Christ from the dead will also give life to your mortal bodies through His Spirit who dwells in you.

Ephesians 1:13-14 AMP
In Him, you also, when you heard the word of truth, the good news of your salvation, and [as a result] believed in Him, were stamped with the seal of the promised Holy

Spirit [the One promised by Christ] as owned and protected [by God]. The Spirit is the guarantee [the first installment, the pledge, a foretaste] of our inheritance until the redemption of God's own [purchased] possession [His believers], to the praise of His glory.

THE POWER OF PRAYER

Jesus said that men should pray always and not lose heart. Prayer is a conversation that may be mental (thought), verbal, or written, between you and God. It is the acknowledgement of God and of His being God. It is our means by which knowledge, understanding, and intimacy in a relationship begin, and of who God is. When we enter into prayer, we are entering into the very presence of God, inviting Him into our situation, where God has our attention, and we have His. Tony Evans defines prayer in his book, The Prayer for Spiritual Power says, "It is the divinely authorized methodology to access heavenly authority for earthly intervention. God established prayer as the primary means to draw down from heaven into history."

Psalm 107:28-30 ESV
Then they cried to the Lord in their trouble, and he delivered them from their distress. He made the storm be still, and the waves of the sea were hushed. Then they were

glad that the waters were quiet, and he brought them to their desired haven.

1 Thessalonians 5:16-18 NLT
Always be joyful. Never stop praying. Be thankful in all circumstances, for this is God's will for you who belong to Christ Jesus.

Psalm 149:5-6 KJV
Let the saints be joyful in glory: let them sing aloud upon their beds. Let the high praises of God be in their mouth, and a two-edged sword in their hand.

Jeremiah 29:11-13 NIV
For I know the plans I have for you, declares the Lord, plans to prosper you and not to harm you, plans to give you hope and a future. Then you will call on me and come and pray to me, and I will listen to you. You will seek me and find me when you seek me with all your heart.

Hebrews 4:16 KJV
Let us therefore come boldly unto the throne of grace that we may obtain mercy, and find grace to help in time of need.

Matthew 21:22 ESV
And whatever you ask in prayer, you will receive, if you have faith.

1 John 5:14-15 NKJV
Now this is the confidence that we have in Him, that if we ask anything according to His will, He hears us. And if we know that He hears us, whatever we ask, we know that we have the petitions that we have asked of Him.

Mark 11:24 ESV
Therefore, I tell you, whatever you ask in prayer, believe that you have received it, and it will be yours.

Philippians 4:6-7 ESV
Do not be anxious about anything, but in everything by prayer and supplication with thanksgiving let your requests be made

known to God. And the peace of God, which surpasses all understanding, will guard your hearts and your minds in Christ Jesus.

John 14:13-14 ESV
Whatever you ask in my name, this I will do, that the Father may be glorified in the Son. If you ask me anything in my name, I will do it.

1 Timothy 2:5 MSG
There's one God and only one, and one Priest-Mediator between God and us – Jesus, who offered himself.

Psalm 61:1-4 NJKV
Hear my cry, O God; Attend my prayer. From the end of the earth I will cry to You, When my heart is overwhelmed; Lead me to the rock that is higher than I. For You have been a shelter for me, A strong tower from the enemy. I will abide in your tabernacle forever; I will trust in the shelter of Your wings. Selah.

Matthew 17:17-21 NKJV

Then Jesus answered and said, "O faithless and perverse generation, how long shall I be with you? How long shall I bear with you? Bring him here to Me." And Jesus rebuked the demon, and it came out of him; and the child was cured from that very hour. Then the disciples came to Jesus privately and said, "Why could we not cast it out?" So Jesus said to them, "Because of your unbelief; for assuredly, I say to you, if you have faith as a mustard seed, you will say to this mountain, 'Move from here to there,' and it will move; and nothing will be impossible for you. However, this kind does not go out except by prayer and fasting."

WALKING WITH GOD

Walking with God is moving with Him in agreement with His will and ways. The Word of God says, "Can two walk together, unless they are agreed." It is when your life is anchored in God, striving to live that which is reflective of the concepts and precepts of the word of God.

Genesis 17:1 AMP
When Abram was ninety-nine years old, the Lord appeared to him and said, I am the Almighty God; walk and live habitually before Me and be perfect (blameless, wholehearted, complete).

Genesis 24:40 ESV
But he said to me, 'The Lord, before whom I have walked, will send his angel with you and prosper your way. You shall take a wife for my son from my clan and from my father's house.

Genesis 48:15 AMP
Then [Jacob] blessed Joseph and said, God [Himself], before Whom my fathers

Abraham and Isaac lived and walked habitually, God [Himself], Who has [been my Shepherd and has led and] fed me from the time I came into being until this day.

2 Corinthians 6:16 KJV
And what agreement hath the temple of God with idols? for ye are the temple of the living God; as God hath said, I will dwell in them, and walk in them; and I will be their God, and they shall be my people.

Micah 6:8 NLT
No, O people, the Lord has told you what is good, and this is what he requires of you: to do what is right, to love mercy, and to walk humbly with your God.

Galatians 5:22-23a NLT
But the Holy Spirit produces this kind of fruit in our lives: love, joy, peace, patience, kindness, goodness, faithfulness, gentleness, and self-control.

Psalm 19:14 NLT
May the words of my mouth and the meditation of my heart be pleasing to You, O Lord, my rock and my redeemer.

1 Corinthians 10:31 ESV
So, whether you eat or drink, or whatever you do, do all to the glory of God.

Psalm 37:23-24 NLT
The Lord directs the steps of the godly. He delights in every detail of their lives. Though they stumble, they will never fall, For the Lord holds them by the hand.

Romans 12:2 NLT
Don't *(conform)* copy the behavior and customs of this world, but let God transform you into a new person by changing the way you think. Then you will learn to know God's will for you, which is good, pleasing, and perfect.

James 4:7 ESV
Submit yourselves therefore to God. Resist the devil, and he will flee from you.

Micah 6:8 ESV
He has told you, O man, what is good; and what does the Lord require of you but to do justice, and to love kindness, and to walk humbly with your God?

Psalm 119:133 ESV
Keep steady my steps according to your promise, and let no iniquity get dominion over me.

Ephesians 2:10 ESV
For we are his workmanship, created in Christ Jesus for good works, which God prepared beforehand, that we should walk in them.

Romans 13:13 ESV
Let us walk properly as in the daytime, not in orgies and drunkenness, not in sexual immorality and sensuality, not in quarreling and jealousy.

James 4:8a NKJV
Draw near to God, and He will draw near to you.

Psalm 65:4 AMP
Blessed is the one whom You choose and bring near to dwell in Your courts. We will be filled with the goodness of Your house, Your holy temple.

Psalm 145:18 AMPC
The Lord is near to all who call upon Him, to all who call upon Him sincerely and in truth.

Forgiving Others and Releasing Ourselves

The definition of forgiveness is the act of pardoning, to excuse a mistake or offense. The greatest act of forgiveness was demonstrated on the cross by Jesus Christ. The price He paid to redeem us back to the Father, which removed every sin that separated us from Him. Unforgiveness has consequences: spiritually, if we do not forgive, our Heavenly Father will not forgive us, and we are separated from God again. And physically, it can cause high blood pressure, ulcers, migraines, backaches, heart attacks, and depression, to name a few. Forgiveness can be a process because of the pain involved, but it can be accomplished with the help and work of the Holy Spirit.

Colossians 3:13 NLT
Make allowance for each other's faults,
and forgive anyone who offends you.
Remember, the Lord forgave you, so
you must forgive others.

Matthew 26:8 ESV
This is my blood of the covenant, which is poured out for many for the forgiveness of sins.

Ezekiel 36:26 NLT
And I will give you a new heart, and I will put a new spirit in you. I will take out your stony, stubborn heart and give you a tender, responsive heart.

1 Thessalonians 5:15-18 ESV
See that no one repays anyone evil for evil, but always seek to do good to one another and to everyone. Rejoice always, pray without ceasing, give thanks in all circumstances; for this is the will of God in Christ Jesus for you.

Ephesians 4:31-32 NIV
Get rid of all bitterness, rage, and anger, brawling and slander, along with every form of malice. Be kind and compassionate to one another, forgiving each other, just as in Christ God forgave you.

When we forgive others, we allow ourselves to be forgiven too

Matthew 6:14-15 ESV
For if you forgive others their trespasses, your heavenly Father will also forgive you, but if you do not forgive others their trespasses, neither will your Father forgive your trespasses.

Matthew 18:21-22 NKJK
Then Peter came to Him and said, Lord, how often shall my brother sin against me, and I forgive him? Up to seven times? Jesus said to him, I do not say to you, up to seven times, but up to seventy times seven.

Proverbs 17:9 NLT
Love prospers when a fault is forgiven, but dwelling on it separates close friends.

Isaiah 43:18 NIV
Forget the former things; do not dwell on the past. See, I am doing a new thing!

1 Peter 3:7 AMP
In the same way you married men should live considerately with [your wives], with an intelligent recognition [of the marriage relation], honoring the woman as [physically] the weaker, but [realizing that you] are joint heirs of the grace (God's unmerited favor) of life, in order that your prayers may not be hindered and cut off. [Otherwise, you cannot pray effectively].

Matthew 18:15 ESV
If your brother sins against you, go and tell him his fault, between you and him alone. If he listens to you, you have gained your brother.

1 John 1:9 ESV
If we confess our sins, he is faithful and just and will forgive us our sins and purify us from all unrighteousness.

Jeremiah 31:34 ESV
No longer will they teach their neighbor,

or say to one another, 'Know the Lord,' because they will all know me, from the least of them to the greatest," declares the Lord. "For I will forgive their wickedness and will remember their sins no more."

Psalm 103:12 ESV
As far as the east is from the west, so far has he removed our transgressions from us.

2 Corinthians 5:18-19 KJV
And all things are of God, who hath reconciled us to himself by Jesus Christ, and hath given to us the ministry of reconciliation; To wit, that God was in Christ, reconciling the world unto himself, not imputing their trespasses unto them; and hath committed unto us the word of reconciliation.

HONORING GOD

Who is like our God, deserving all the praise and glory as we reverently fear and honor Him in all of His Holiness in action, as we keep His Word! The Greek word is "timáō" meaning to prize, i.e., fix a valuation upon; by implication, to revere:–honour, value. What is the value of your relationship with God?

1 John 3:22 ESV
And whatever we ask we receive from him, because we keep his commandments and do what pleases him.

John 15:7 ESV
If you abide in me, and my words abide in you, ask whatever you wish, and it will be done for you.

Psalm 105:4 NIV
Look to the Lord and his strength; seek his face always.

2 Chronicles 16:9a NKJV
For the eyes of the Lord run to and fro throughout the whole earth, to show Himself strong on behalf of those whose heart is loyal to Him.

1 Peter 4:11 NIV
If anyone speaks, he should do it as one speaking the very words of God. If anyone serves, he should do it with the strength God provides, so that in all things God may be praised through Jesus Christ. To him be the glory and the power forever and ever. Amen.

Psalm 103:2 NLT
Let all that I am praise the Lord; may I never forget the good things he does for me.

Psalm 100:4 ESV
Enter his gates with thanksgiving, and his courts with praise! Give thanks to him; bless his name!

Psalms 92:1-4 NKJV
It is good to give thanks to the Lord, and to sing praises to Your name, O Most High; To declare Your lovingkindness in the morning, and Your faithfulness every night, on an instrument of ten strings, on the lute, and on the harp, with harmonious sound. For You, Lord, have made me glad through Your work; I will triumph in the works of Your hands.

Colossians 3:17 NKJV
And whatever you do, in word or deed, do everything in the name of the Lord Jesus, giving thanks to God the Father through him.

Proverbs 3:9 NKJV
Honor the Lord with your possessions, and with the firstfruits of all your increase.

1 Corinthians 6:20 NKJV
For you were bought at a price; therefore glorify God in your body and in your spirit, which are God's.

1 Corinthians 10:31 TPT
Whether you eat or drink, live your life in a way that glorifies and honors God.

1 Samuel 2:30 ESV
Therefore, the Lord, the God of Israel, declares: "I promised that your house and the house of your father should go in and out before me forever," but now the Lord declares: "Far be it from me, for those who honor me I will honor, and those who despise me shall be lightly esteemed."

Deuteronomy 6:5 ESV
You shall love the Lord your God with all your heart and with all your soul and with all your might.

1 Corinthians 3:16 ESV
Do you not know that you are God's temple and that God's Spirit dwells in you?

TRUSTING IN GOD

God is not a man, that he should lie; neither the son of man, that he should repent: hath he said, and shall he not do it? Or hath he spoken, and shall he not make it good (Numbers 23:19 KJV)? Trusting God comes from spending time with Him to develop a relationship with Him. Who can trust someone they don't know? Trust is to believe, rely on, depend on, because of one's proven character. He is an unchangeable God whom you can depend upon. "For when God made a promise to Abraham, because He could swear by no one greater, He swore by Himself." Hebrews 6:13

Proverbs 3:5-6 ESV
Trust in the Lord with all your heart, and do not lean on your own understanding. In all your ways acknowledge him, and he will make straight your paths.

Romans 15:13 NLT
I pray that God, the source of hope, will fill you completely with joy and peace because

you trust in him. Then you will overflow with confident hope through the power of the Holy Spirit.

Psalm 27:1 NLT
The Lord is my light and my salvation; whom shall I fear? The Lord is the stronghold of my life; of whom shall I be afraid?

Isaiah 41:10 13 NLT
Don't be afraid, for I am with you. Don't be discouraged, for I am your God. I will strengthen you and help you. I will hold you up with my victorious right hand. For I hold you by your right hand – I, the Lord your God. And I say to you, Don't be afraid. I am here to help you.

Psalm 9:10 NLT
Those who know your name trust in you, for you, O Lord, do not abandon those who search for you.

Psalm 118:8 KJV
It is better to trust in the Lord than to put confidence in man.

Psalm 31:14-15 NKJV
But as for me, I trust in You, O Lord; I say, "You are my God." My times are in Your hand; Deliver me from the hand of my enemies, and from those who persecute me.

Psalm 20: 7-8 NIV
Some trust in chariots and some in horses, but we trust in the name of the Lord our God. They are brought to their knees and fall, but we rise up and stand firm.

Jeremiah 32:27 NASB
Behold, I am the Lord, the God of all flesh; is anything too difficult for Me?

Psalm 22:4 KJV
Our fathers trusted in thee: they trusted, and thou didst deliver them.

Nehemiah 1:10 NIV
They are your servants and your people, whom you redeemed by your great strength and your mighty hand.

Romans 15:13 NIV
May the God of hope fill you with all joy and peace as you trust in him, so that you may overflow with hope by the power of the Holy Spirit.

PEACE

What a wonderful part of the Fruit of the Spirit. This kind of peace is only through our relationship in Jesus Christ, which the world is incapable of giving to you. It surpasses human reasoning and understanding, bringing you into a spiritual tranquility of calm, rest, and contentment amid everything happening around you and to you.

John 14:26-27 NIV
But the Advocate, the Holy Spirit, whom the Father will send in my name, will teach you all things and will remind you of everything I have said to you. Peace I leave with you; my peace I give you. I do not give to you as the world gives. Do not let your hearts be troubled and do not be afraid.

Philippians 4:6-7 AMP
Do not be anxious or worried about anything, but in everything [every circumstance and situation] by prayer

and petition with thanksgiving, continue to make your [specific] requests known to God. And the peace of God [that peace which reassures the heart, that peace] which transcends all understanding, [that peace which] stands guard over your hearts and your minds in Christ Jesus [is yours].

Psalm 29:11 AMPC
The Lord will give [unyielding and impenetrable] strength to His people; the Lord will bless His people with peace.

Isaiah 9:6 NKJV
For unto us a Child is born, Unto us a Son is given; And the government will be upon His shoulder. And His name will be called Wonderful, Counselor, Mighty God, Everlasting Father, Prince of Peace.

Psalm 37:37 NKJV
Mark the blameless man, and observe the upright; For the future of that man is peace.

Psalm 34:12-14 NKJV
Who is the man who desires life, and loves many days, that he may see good? Keep your tongue from evil, and your lips from speaking deceit. Depart from evil and do good; Seek peace and pursue it.

Psalm 4:8 AMPC
In peace I will both lie down and sleep, for You, Lord, alone make me dwell in safety and confident trust.

Isaiah 26:3 NKJV
You will keep him in perfect peace, whose mind is stayed on You, because he trusts in You.

2 Thessalonians 3:16 AMPC
Now may the Lord of peace Himself grant you His peace (the peace of His kingdom) at all times and in all ways [under all circumstances and conditions, whatever comes]. The Lord be with you all.

John 16:33 KJV
These things I have spoken unto you, that in me ye might have peace. In the world ye shall have tribulation: but be of good cheer; I have overcome the world.

Galatians 5:22-23 KJV
But the fruit of the Spirit is love, joy, peace, longsuffering, gentleness, goodness, faith, meekness, temperance: against such there is no law.

Matthew 5:9 KJV
Blessed are the peacemakers: for they shall be called the children of God.

Romans 12:18 ESV
If possible, so far as it depends on you, live peaceably with all.

Colossians 3:15 KJV
And let the peace of God rule in your hearts, to which also ye are called in one body; and be ye thankful.

1 Peter 3:11 NKJV
Let him turn away from evil and do good;
Let him seek peace and pursue it.

Romans 8:6 KJV
For to be carnally minded is death; but to be spiritually minded is life and peace.

Psalm 119:165 KJV
Great peace have they which love thy law: and nothing shall offend them.

Isaiah 26:12 NIV
Lord, you establish peace for us; all that we have accomplished, you have done for us.

James 3:18 KJV
And the fruit of righteousness is sown in peace of them that make peace.

THE FAITHFULNESS OF GOD

God's fidelity, His devotion and loyalty to us, is steadfast.

Proverbs 18:10 NKJV
The name of the Lord is a strong tower;
The righteous run to it and are safe.

Psalm 119:105 ESV
Your word is a lamp to my feet and a light to my path.

Psalm 119:133 ESV
Keep steady my steps according to your promise, and let no iniquity get dominion over me.

Jeremiah 29:11 ESV
For I know the plans I have for you," declares the Lord, "plans to prosper you and not to harm you, plans to give you hope and a future.

Psalm 94:20-23 NKJV
Shall the throne of iniquity, which devises evil by law, have fellowship with You? They gather together against the life of the righteous and condemn innocent blood.
But the Lord has been my defense, and my God the rock of my refuge. He has brought on them their own iniquity, and shall cut them off in their own wickedness;
The Lord our God shall cut them off.

Hebrews 6:10 TPT
For God, the Faithful One, is not unfair. How can he forget the work you have done for him? He remembers the love you demonstrate as you continually serve his beloved ones for the glory of his name.

1 Corinthians 1:9 AMPC
God is faithful (reliable, trustworthy, and therefore ever true to His promise, and He can be depended on); by Him you were called into companionship *and* participation with His Son, Jesus Christ our Lord.

I John 5:14-15 AMPC
And this is the confidence (the assurance, the privilege of boldness) which we have in Him: [we are sure] that if we ask anything (make any request) according to His will (in agreement with His own plan), He listens to and hears us. And if (since) we [positively] know that He listens to us in whatever we ask, we also know [with settled and absolute knowledge] that we have [granted us as our present possessions] the requests made of Him.

Deuteronomy 7:9 ESV
Know therefore that the Lord your God is God, the faithful God who keeps covenant and steadfast love with those who love him and keep his commandments, to a thousand generations.

Psalm 36:5 KJV
Thy mercy, O Lord, is in the heavens; and thy faithfulness reacheth unto the clouds.

1 Corinthians 10:13 ESV
No temptation has overtaken you that is not common to man. God is faithful, and He will not let you be tempted beyond your ability, but with the temptation he will also provide a way of escape, that you may be able to endure it.

2 Thessalonians 3:3 KJV
But the Lord is faithful, who shall stablish you, and keep you from evil.

Hebrews 10:23 NKJV
Let us hold fast the confession of our hope without wavering, for He who promised is faithful.

Romans 3:3 NKJV
For what if some did not believe? Will their unbelief make the faithfulness of God without effect?

1 Corinthians 1:9 AMP
God is faithful [He is reliable, trustworthy, and ever true to His promise—He can be depended on], and through Him you were

called into fellowship with His Son, Jesus Christ our Lord.

Lamentations 3:22-23 KJV
It is of the Lord's mercies that we are not consumed, because his compassions fail not. They are new every morning: great is thy faithfulness.

Psalm 89:8 ESV
O Lord God of hosts, who is mighty as you are, O Lord, with your faithfulness all around you?

FAITH

- *"Faith is seeing light with your heart when all your eyes see is darkness."*
- *"Faith, it's all about believing, you don't know how it will happen, but you know it will."*
- *"Let your faith be bigger than your fear."*
- *"Faith is taking the first step even when you don't see the whole staircase."*
- *"Your faith can move mountains, and your doubt can create them."*

2 Corinthians 5:7 ESV
For we walk by faith, not by sight.

Romans 10:17 ESV
So faith comes from hearing, and hearing through the word of Christ.

Ephesians 2:8–9 NIV
For it is by grace you have been saved, through faith—and this is not from

yourselves, it is the gift of God, not by works, so that no one can boast.

Hebrew 11:1 AMPC
Now faith is the assurance (the confirmation, the title deed) of the things [we] hope for, being the proof of things [we] do not see and the conviction of their reality [faith perceiving as real fact what is not revealed to the senses].

Hebrew 11:3 NKJV
By faith we understand that the worlds were framed by the word of God, so that the things which are seen were not made of things which are visible.

Hebrews 11:6 NJKV
But without faith it is impossible to please Him, for he who comes to God must believe that He is, and that He is a rewarder of those who diligently seek Him.

1 John 5:4-5 AMP
For everyone born of God is victorious

and overcomes the world; and this is the victory that has conquered and overcome the world—our [continuing, persistent] faith [in Jesus the Son of God]. Who is the one who is victorious and overcomes the world? It is the one who believes and recognizes the fact that Jesus is the Son of God.

Jude 3:3 NKJV
Beloved, while I was very diligent to write to you concerning our common salvation, I found it necessary to write to you exhorting you to contend earnestly for the faith which was once for all delivered to the saints.

Jude 1:20 NKJV
But you, beloved, building yourselves up on your most holy faith, praying in the Holy Spirit.

James 1:6-7 KJV
But let him ask in faith, nothing wavering. For he that wavereth is like a wave of the sea driven with the wind and tossed. For

let not that man think that he shall receive anything of the Lord.

Romans 1:17 NKJV
For in it (the gospel) the righteousness of God is revealed from faith to faith; as it is written: "The just shall live by faith."

Matthew 17:20 NIV
He replied, "Because you have so little faith. Truly I tell you, if you have faith as small as a mustard seed, you can say to this mountain, 'Move from here to there,' and it will move. Nothing will be impossible for you."

Hebrews 11:30 ESV
By faith, the walls of Jericho fell after the army had marched around them for seven days.

Matthew 21:22 ESV
And whatever you ask in prayer, you will receive, if you have faith.

Psalm 62:5 KJV
My soul, wait thou only upon God; for my expectation is from him.

Proverbs 3:5-6 KJV
Trust in the Lord with all thine heart; and lean not unto thine own understanding. In all thy ways acknowledge him, and he shall direct thy paths.

ENCOURAGEMENT

Revelation 22:13, "I am the Alpha and the Omega, the Beginning and the End, the First and the Last." He is your Before all and the End of all, and He is even in the middle of it all. Therefore, He can direct your day and make it successful. He will speak to you when you don't know what decision to make or what to do next, especially when your days are long, and your strength is going/gone. There is a scripture in Isaiah that says, "Your ears shall hear a word behind you saying, 'This is the way, walk in it, whenever you turn to the right hand or whenever you turn to the left." Allow Him to be the beginning of your day and thank Him at the end of it. He is with you! And because He knows the beginning from the end, He has the solution, problem-solving skills, along with the power to get you through any situation or circumstance. So, with all of this, the confidence comes from knowing He has your back.

1 Corinthians 1:9 TPT
God is faithful (reliable, trustworthy, and therefore ever true to His promise, and He can be depended on); by Him you were called into companionship *and* participation with His Son, Jesus Christ our Lord.

Hebrews 10:23 AMP
Let us seize and hold tightly the confession of our hope without wavering, for He who promised is reliable and trustworthy and faithful [to His word].

> **To seize and hold tightly** means to hold fast, keep secure, and keep firm possession of.
>
> **The Confession of your hope**, that is, to declare or acknowledge with confidence.

Confess what you want to see because in our tongues we have the power to speak life and death over any situation. Do not be confounded by what you see, but by what you know of God, and that He is a

God of miracles. Do this without wavering, being double-minded, because a double-minded person receives nothing from God (James 1:6-8). The Word of God is a lamp to our feet and a light to our path (see also Proverbs 6:22). Therefore, it is the light by which we are to live. Jesus Christ, The Light of the world, and The Living Word, will bring light into every area of your life so that you may see the manifestation of the Father's promises.

John 15:7 KJV
If ye abide in me, and my words abide in you, ye shall ask what ye will, and it shall be done unto you.

Ephesians 3:20-21 AMP
He Who promised is reliable and trustworthy and faithful [to His word], He is able to do exceeding abundantly above all that you can imagine or hope or dream according to the power that works in us. He has the power to get you through this and answer your prayers concerning your family, job, and your needs. He has

not forgotten you and your sacrifices, nor your concerns.

Hebrews 11:6 AMP
But without faith it is impossible to [walk with God and] please Him, for whoever comes [near] to God must [necessarily] believe that God exists and that He rewards those who [earnestly and diligently] seek Him.

Deuteronomy 20:4 NIV
For the Lord your God is the one who goes with you to fight for you against your enemies to give you victory.

Psalm 59:16 KJV
But I will sing of thy power; yea, I will sing aloud of thy mercy in the morning: for thou hast been my defence and refuge in the day of my trouble.

Joshua 1:9 KJV
Have not I commanded thee? Be strong and of good courage; be not afraid, neither

be thou dismayed: for the Lord thy God is with thee whithersoever thou goest.

Psalm 62:6-8 AMP
He only is my rock and my salvation; My fortress and my defense, I will not be shaken or discouraged. On God my salvation and my glory rest; He is my rock of [unyielding] strength, my refuge is in God. Trust [confidently] in Him at all times, O people; Pour out your heart before Him. God is a refuge for us. Selah.

Isaiah 41:10 AMP
Do not fear [anything], for I am with you; Do not be afraid, for I am your God. I will strengthen you, be assured I will help you; I will certainly take hold of you with My righteous right hand [a hand of justice, of power, of victory, of salvation].

He says, do not look around you in terror and be dismayed during this time and season, for He is your God. He will strengthen and comfort you through the difficulties of these times we are now in.

He will make you stronger because you will be operating in His strength, not yours. He gives strength to the weak and increases power to those who have no might in daily duties at work and at home. And to be assured means He has made a promise to help you, and He is not changing His mind because of His great love He has for you. His word is true, and He cannot deny Himself. A God who could not find anyone greater than Himself to swear by, so He swore by Himself.

So don't be dismayed (alarm, anxious, disheartened, discouraged, panic), be at peace and be encouraged in the Lord. He is with you and has given His angels charge of you to keep you in all your ways.

Ephesians 2:10 NKJV
For we are his workmanship, created in Christ Jesus for good works, which God prepared beforehand, that we should walk in them.

Ephesians 2:10 AMPC
For we are God's [own] handiwork (His workmanship), recreated in Christ Jesus, [born anew] that we may do those good works which God predestined (planned beforehand) for us [taking paths which He prepared ahead of time], that we should walk in them [living the good life which He prearranged and made ready for us to live].

Philippians 4:13 KJV
I can do all things through Christ, which strengtheneth me.

Psalm 27:1 KJV
The Lord is my light and my salvation; whom shall I fear? The Lord is the strength of my life; of whom shall I be afraid?

Psalm 29:11 AMP
The Lord will give [unyielding and impenetrable] strength to His people; The Lord will bless His people with peace.

Psalm 73:26 KJV
My flesh and my heart faileth: but God is the strength of my heart, and my portion forever.

Psalm 18:1-2 NKJV
I will love You, O Lord, my strength. The Lord is my rock and my fortress and my deliverer; My God, my strength, in whom I will trust; My shield and the horn of my salvation, my stronghold.

2 Corinthians 12:9-10 NIV
But he said to me, "My grace is sufficient for you, for my power is made perfect in weakness." Therefore, I will boast all the more gladly about my weaknesses, so that Christ's power may rest on me. That is why, for Christ's sake, I delight in weaknesses, in insults, in hardships, in persecutions, in difficulties. For when I am weak, then I am strong.

Ephesians 3:16 KJV
That he would grant you, according to the riches of his glory, to be strengthened with might by his Spirit in the inner man.

Isaiah 33:2 KJV
O Lord, be gracious unto us; we have waited for thee: be thou their arm every morning, our salvation also in the time of trouble.

Romans 15:13 TPT
Now may God, the fountain of hope, fill you to overflowing with uncontainable joy and perfect peace as you trust in him. And may the power of the Holy Spirit continually surround your life with his super-abundance until you radiate with hope!

Psalm 18:28-30 ESV
For it is you who light my lamp; the Lord my God lightens my darkness. For by you I can run against a troop, and by my God I can leap over a wall. This God—his way is perfect; the word of the Lord proves true;

He is a shield for all those who take refuge in Him.

SALVATION

How shall we escape, if we neglect so great salvation
James 2:3 KJV

2 Corinthians 5:17 ESV
Therefore, if anyone is in Christ, he is a new creation. The old has passed away; behold, the new has come.

Ephesians 5:8 ESV
For at one time you were darkness, but now you are light in the Lord. Walk as children of light.

Hebrews 12:1 ESV
Therefore, since we are surrounded by so great a cloud of witnesses, let us also lay aside every weight, and sin which clings so closely, and let us run with endurance the race that is set before us.

Hebrews 9:14 KJV
How much more shall the blood of Christ, who through the eternal Spirit offered

himself without spot to God, purge your conscience from dead works to serve the living God?

Hebrews 10:12 NKJV
But this Man, after He had offered one sacrifice for sins forever, sat down at the right hand of God.

Romans 10:8-14 NKJV
But what does it say? "The word is near you, in your mouth and in your heart," (that is, the word of faith which we preach) that if you confess with your mouth the Lord Jesus and believe in your heart that God has raised Him from the dead, you will be saved. For with the heart one believes unto righteousness, and with the mouth confession is made unto salvation. For the Scripture says, "Whoever believes on Him will not be put to shame." For there is no distinction between Jew and Greek, for the same Lord over all is rich to all who call upon Him. For "whoever calls on the name of the Lord shall be saved." How then shall they call on Him in whom they have not

believed? And how shall they believe in Him of whom they have not heard? And how shall they hear without a preacher?

Ephesians 2:8–9 NIV
For it is by grace you have been saved, through faith—and this is not from yourselves, it is the gift of God, not by works, so that no one can boast.

Romans 1:16-17 KJV
For I am not ashamed of the gospel of Christ: for it is the power of God unto salvation to every one that believeth; to the Jew first, and also to the Greek. For therein is the righteousness of God revealed from faith to faith: as it is written, the just shall live by faith.

1 John 5:10-13 NKJV
He who believes in the Son of God has the witness in himself; he who does not believe God has made Him a liar, because he has not believed the testimony that God has given of His Son. And this is the testimony: that God has given us eternal life, and this

life is in His Son. He who has the Son has life; he who does not have the Son of God does not have life. These things I have written to you who believe in the name of the Son of God, that you may know that you have eternal life, and that you may continue to believe in the name of the Son of God.

1 John 5:20 NKJV
And we know that the Son of God has come and has given us an understanding, that we may know Him who is true; and we are in Him who is true, in His Son Jesus Christ. This is the true God and eternal life.

Acts 4:12 NKJV
Nor is there salvation in any other, for there is no other name under heaven given among men by which we must be saved.

John 17:9 NKJV
I pray for them. I do not pray for the world but for those whom You have given Me, for they are Yours.

1 Corinthians 1:18 NKJV
For the message of the cross is foolishness to those who are perishing, but to us who are being saved it is the power of God.

Mark 16:15-18 NKJV
And He said to them, "Go into all the world and preach the gospel to every creature. He who believes and is baptized will be saved; but he who does not believe will be condemned. And these signs will follow those who believe: In My name they will cast out demons; they will speak with new tongues; they will take up serpents; and if they drink anything deadly, it will by no means hurt them; they will lay hands on the sick, and they will recover."

Romans 7:4 ESV
Likewise, my brothers, you also have died to the law through the body of Christ, so that you may belong to another, to him who has been raised from the dead, in order that we may bear fruit for God.

Hebrews 2:3 LB
What makes us think that we can escape if we are indifferent to this great salvation announced by the Lord Jesus himself and passed on to us by those who heard him speak?

2 Corinthians 5:20-21 NKJV
Now then, we are ambassadors for Christ, as though God were pleading through us: we implore you on Christ's behalf, be reconciled to God. For He made Him who knew no sin to be sin for us, that we might become the righteousness of God in Him.

HEALING

In the Old Testament the word "rapa" meant to heal or to cure, whether in the physical nature or that of a nation. It can also mean to restore to the normal state. Jehovah Rapha is the "God Who Heals," demonstrating His healing and restoring power throughout His Word. His grace and forgiveness to Israel were extended as they returned to Him from their sins with repentant hearts. This same grace and mercy are still available to us. I John 1:9 says, "If we confess our sins, he is faithful and just and will forgive us our sins and purify us from all unrighteousness." In the New Testament, God provided for us His Son, Jesus Christ, as our Healer. In the New Testament, the word "sozo/diasozo translated means to heal, to save, or to save thoroughly. Jesus not only healed our physical being, but also provided for us eternal salvation, the gift of everlasting life. What a price that was paid for our complete wholeness of spirit, soul, and body!

Isaiah 53:4-5 NKJV
Surely He has borne our griefs [sickness] And carried our sorrows [pains]; Yet we esteemed [reckoned] Him stricken, Smitten [Struck down] by God, and afflicted. But He was wounded [pierced through] for our transgressions, He was bruised [crushed] for our iniquities. The chastisement for our peace was upon Him, and by His stripes [Blows that cut in] we are healed.

God did not reject Christ. He rejected the sins that were placed on Christ. Jesus cried out My God, My God, why hast Thou forsaken Me? (Books of Matthew and Mark)

Luke 23:46 NKJV
And when Jesus had cried out with a loud voice, He said, "Father, into Your hands I commit My spirit." Having said this, He breathed His last.

Romans 6:5 NKJV
For if we have been united together in the likeness of His death, certainly we also

shall be in the_likeness of His resurrection.

Romans 6:4 NKJV
Therefore, we were buried with Him through baptism into death, that just as Christ was raised from the dead by the glory of the Father [And God both raised up the Lord and will also raise us up by His power].

> Even so, we also should walk in the newness of life [See Romans 7:6, 2 Corinthians 5:17, *Galatians 6:15, Ephesians 4:23, Colossians 3:10].*

Romans 6:6-13 NKJV
Knowing this, that our old man was crucified with Him, that the body of sin might be done away with, that we should no longer be slaves of sin. For he who has died has been freed from sin. Now if we died with Christ, we believe that we shall also live with Him, knowing that Christ, having been raised from the dead, dies no more. Death no longer has dominion over

Him. For the death that He died, He died to sin once for all; but the life that He lives, He lives to God. Likewise, you also reckon yourselves to be dead indeed to sin, but alive to God in Christ Jesus our Lord. Therefore, do not let sin reign in your mortal body, that you should obey it in its lusts. And do not present your members as instruments of unrighteousness to sin, but present yourselves to God as being alive from the dead, and your members as instruments of righteousness to God.

James 5:14-16 ESV
Is anyone among you sick? Let him call for the elders of the church, and let them pray over him, anointing him with oil in the name of the Lord. And the prayer of faith will save the one who is sick, and the Lord will raise him up. And if he has committed sins, he will be forgiven. Therefore, confess your sins to one another and pray for one another, that you may be healed. The prayer of a righteous person has great power as it is working.

Psalm 107:19-20 NASB
Then they cried out to the Lord in their trouble; He saved them out of their distress. He sent His word and healed them, and delivered them from their destruction.

Psalm 147:3 NASB
He heals the brokenhearted and binds up their wounds.

Psalm 41:3 AMP
The Lord will sustain and strengthen him on his sickbed; In his illness, You will restore him to health.

1 John 5:14-15 NKJV
Now this is the confidence that we have in Him, that if we ask anything according to His will, He hears us. And if we know that He hears us, whatever we ask, we know that we have the petitions that we have asked of Him.

Proverbs 4:20-22 NLT
My child, pay attention to what I say. Listen carefully to my words. Don't lose sight of them. Let them penetrate deep into your heart. For they bring life to those who find them, and healing to their whole body.

Isaiah 54:17 KJV
No weapon that is formed against thee shall prosper; and every tongue that shall rise against thee in judgment thou shalt condemn. This is the heritage of the servants of the Lord, and their righteousness is of me, saith the Lord.

Psalm 103:1-5 NKJV
Bless the Lord, O my soul; And all that is within me, bless His holy name! Bless the Lord, O my soul, And forget not all His benefits: Who forgives all your iniquities, Who heals all your diseases. Who redeems your life from destruction, Who crowns you with lovingkindness and tender mercies. Who satisfies your mouth with good things, so that your youth is renewed like the eagle's.

Jeremiah 17:14 NKJV
Heal me, O Lord, and I shall be healed; Save me, and I shall be saved, For you are my praise.

Matthew 15:26-28 NKJV
But He answered and said, "It is not good to take the children's bread and throw it to the little dogs." And she said, "Yes, Lord, yet even the little dogs eat the crumbs which fall from their masters' table." Then Jesus answered and said to her, "O woman, great is your faith! Let it be to you as you desire." And her daughter was healed from that very hour.

HEALING IS THE CHILDREN'S BREAD

As children of God, healing is our right. It is our life-given right that has already been provided for us through the life, death, and resurrection of Jesus Christ. God has promised to heal all of our diseases. His promises are sure. They are yes and amen.

Exodus 23:25-26 NIV
Worship the Lord your God, and his blessing will be on your food and water. I will take away sickness from among you, and none will miscarry or be barren in your land. I will give you a full life span.

Proverbs 17:22 NIV
A cheerful heart is good medicine, but a crushed spirit dries up the bones.

Isaiah 33:2 AMP
O Lord, be gracious to us; we have waited [expectantly] for You. Be the arm of Your servants every morning [that is, their

strength and their defense], our salvation also in the time of trouble.

John 14:27 AMP
Peace I leave with you; My [perfect] peace I give to you; not as the world gives do I give to you. Do not let your heart be troubled, nor let it be afraid. [Let My perfect peace calm you in every circumstance and give you courage and strength for every challenge].

Isaiah 40:29 NIV
He gives strength to the weary and increases the power of the weak.

Psalm 30:2 KJV
O Lord my God, I cried unto thee, and thou hast healed me.

Psalm 73:25-26 KJV
Whom have I in heaven but thee? and there is none upon earth that I desire beside thee. My flesh and my heart faileth: but God is the strength of my heart, and my portion forever.

Acts 17:28 AMP
For in Him we live and move and exist [that is, in Him we actually have our being], as even some of your own poets have said, "For we also are His children."

2 Corinthians 5:18-19 NKJV
Now all things are of God, who has reconciled us to Himself through Jesus Christ, and has given us the ministry of reconciliation, that is, that God was in Christ reconciling the world to Himself, not imputing their trespasses to them, and has committed to us the word of reconciliation.

1 Peter 2:24 ESV
He himself bore our sins in his body on the tree, that we might die to sin and live to righteousness. By his wounds you have been healed.

Psalm 6:2 NLT
Have compassion on me, Lord, for I am weak. Heal me, Lord, for my bones are in agony.

Jeremiah 3:22 NKJV
"Return, you backsliding children, And I will heal your backsliding." Indeed, we do come to You, for You are the Lord our God.

Matthew 11:28-30 NLT
Then Jesus said, "Come to me, all of you who are weary and carry heavy burdens, and I will give you rest. Take my yoke upon you. Let me teach you, because I am humble and gentle at heart, and you will find rest for your souls. For my yoke is easy to bear, and the burden I give you is light."

THE BENEFITS OF SERVING GOD

It is not only an honor and a privilege to serve the Most High God, but that service with a pure heart also comes with benefits. Benefits, meaning "rewards". So, as we delight ourselves in doing His will, God will reward us for our service. What true Father does not generously reward his child for their obedience and loving actions? "Delight yourself also in the Lord, And He shall give you the desires of your heart." Psalms 37:4 NKJV

Hebrews 6:10 NKJV
For God is not unjust to forget your work and labor of love which you have shown toward His name, in that you have ministered to the saints, and minister.

Isaiah 1:19-20 NKJV
If you are willing and obedient, you shall eat the good of the land; But if you refuse and rebel, you shall be devoured by the sword."For the mouth of the Lord has spoken.

John 14:15 TPT
"Loving me empowers you to obey (keep) my commands.

2 Chronicles 16:9a NKJV
For the eyes of the Lord run to and fro throughout the whole earth, to show Himself strong (to give strong support) on behalf of those whose heart is loyal to Him.

1 Samuel 15:22-23 AMPC
Samuel said, Has the Lord as great a delight in burnt offerings and sacrifices as in obeying the voice of the Lord? Behold, to obey is better than sacrifice, and to hearken than the fat of rams. For rebellion is as the sin of witchcraft, and stubbornness is as idolatry and teraphim (household good luck images). Because you have rejected the word of the Lord, He also has rejected you from being king.

Psalm 84:11 AMPC
For the Lord God is a Sun and Shield; the Lord bestows [present] grace and favor

and [future] glory (honor, splendor, and heavenly bliss)! No good thing will He withhold from those who walk uprightly.

James 1:5 ESV
If any of you lacks wisdom, let him ask God, who gives generously to all without reproach, and it will be given to him.

Psalm 145:19 NKJV
He will fulfill the desire of those who fear Him; He also will hear their cry and save them.

Acts 20:35 NKJV
I have shown you in every way, by laboring like this, that you must support the weak. And remember the words of the Lord Jesus, that He said, "It is more blessed to give than to receive."

1 Peter 4:10-11 TPT
Every believer has received grace gifts, so use them to serve one another as faithful stewards of the many-colored tapestry of God's grace. For example, if you have a

speaking gift, speak as though God were speaking his words through you. If you have the gift of serving, do it passionately with the strength God gives you, so that in everything God alone will be glorified through Jesus Christ. For to him belong the power and the glory forever throughout all ages! Amen.

Colossians 3:23-24 KJV
And whatsoever ye do, do it heartily, as to the Lord, and not unto men; knowing that of the Lord ye shall receive the reward of the inheritance: for ye serve the Lord Christ.

1 Corinthians 15:58 KJV
Therefore, my beloved brethren, be ye stedfast, unmoveable, always abounding in the work of the Lord, forasmuch as ye know that your labour is not in vain in the Lord.

John 12:26 KJV
If any man serves me, let him follow me; and where I am, there shall also my

servant be: if any man serves me,
he will my Father honour.

2 Corinthians 9:7 KJV
Every man according as he purposeth in his heart, so let him give; not grudgingly, or of necessity: for God loveth a cheerful giver.

Proverbs 11:25 AMP
The generous man [is a source of blessing and] shall be prosperous and enriched, and he who waters will himself be watered [reaping the generosity he has sown].

1 Timothy 1:12 KJV
And I thank Christ Jesus our Lord, who hath enabled me, for that he counted me faithful, putting me into the ministry.

Psalm 27:5 KJV
For in the time of trouble he shall hide me in his pavilion: in the secret of his tabernacle shall he hide me; he shall set me up upon a rock.

Isaiah 58:13-14 VOICE
Eternal One: If because of the Sabbath you set aside your own pursuits and pleasure, and you honor the Sabbath and sanctify that day by leaving it to and for the Eternal. If you speak of Sabbath-delight but avoid speaking idle words, and refuse to get caught up and busy with your interests and concerns. Then you will discover joy such as only the Eternal can give. And I will raise you high and make your reach as wide as the earth, and you will live on all that I promised to Jacob, your ancestor, the heart of Israel. The Eternal One said these very things.

WISDOM

There are two kinds of wisdom: worldly and godly. James describes worldly wisdom as jealousy and selfishness, which are earthly, unspiritual, and demonic. Yet, godly wisdom is pure, peaceable, and is from above. This type of wisdom enables us to apply the Word of God with understanding, knowledge, and power. The beginning of this wisdom is the fear of God.

James 1:5 ESV
If any of you lacks wisdom, let him ask God, who gives generously to all without reproach, and it will be given to him.

Psalm 111:10 ESV
The fear of the Lord is the beginning of wisdom; all those who practice it have a good understanding. His praise endures forever!

Proverbs 11:30b NKJV
And he who wins souls is wise.

Proverbs 3:35 AMPC
The wise shall inherit glory (all honor and good), but shame is the highest rank conferred on [self-confident] fools.

Daniel 12:3 AMPC
And the teachers and those who are wise shall shine like the brightness of the firmament, and those who turn many to righteousness (to uprightness and right standing with God) [shall give forth light] like the stars forever and ever.

Proverbs 11:2 ESV
When pride comes, then comes disgrace, but with humility comes wisdom.

Proverbs 16:16 NIV
How much better to get wisdom than gold, to get insight rather than silver!

Proverbs 2:6-7 KJV
For the Lord giveth wisdom: out of his mouth cometh knowledge and understanding. He layeth up sound

wisdom for the righteous: he is a buckler to them that walk uprightly.

Ecclesiastes 2:26 NKJV
For God gives wisdom and knowledge and joy to a man who is good in His sight; but to the sinner He gives the work of gathering and collecting, that he may give to him who is good before God. This also is vanity and grasping for the wind.

James 3:17 ESV
But the wisdom from above is first pure, then peaceable, gentle, open to reason, full of mercy and good fruits, impartial and sincere.

Proverbs 19:20 ESV
Listen to advice and accept instruction, that you may gain wisdom in the future.

Proverbs 12:15 ESV
The way of a fool is right in his own eyes, but a wise man listens to advice.

Proverbs 17:27-28 ESV
Whoever restrains his words has knowledge, and he who has a cool spirit is a man of understanding. Even a fool who keeps silent is considered wise; when he closes his lips, he is deemed intelligent.

Proverbs 4:8-9 TPT
Wisdom will exalt you when you exalt her truth. She will lead you to honor and favor when you live your life by her insights. You will be adorned with beauty and grace, and wisdom's glory will wrap itself around you, making you victorious in the race.

Proverbs 4:6-7 ESV
Do not forsake her, and she will keep you; love her, and she will guard you. The beginning of wisdom is this: Get wisdom, and whatever you get, get insight.

Ecclesiastes 7:12 ESV
For the protection of wisdom is like the protection of money, and the advantage of knowledge is that wisdom preserves the life of him who has it.

Colossians 2:8 ESV
See to it that no one takes you captive by philosophy and empty deceit, according to human tradition, according to the elemental spirits of the world, and not according to Christ.

Matthew 7:24 ESV
"Everyone then who hears these words of mine and does them will be like a wise man who built his house on the rock.

Proverbs 29:11 ESV
A fool gives full vent to his spirit, but a wise man quietly holds it back.

Romans 11:33 ESV
Oh, the depth of the riches and wisdom and knowledge of God! How unsearchable are his judgments and how inscrutable his ways!

1 Corinthians 3:18 ESV
Let no one deceive himself. If anyone among you thinks that he is wise in this

age, let him become a fool, that he may become wise.

Comfort in Being Tired, Weary, and Distressed

Jesus said, "Come to me, all of you who are weary and carry heavy burdens, and I will give you rest." Jesus knew that we would have troubles in this world and be fatigued and frustrated by its cares. As we come to Him, keeping our mind on Him and our hope in Him, there we will find a refreshing, quiet place in His Presence.

Isaiah 40:28-31 ESV
Have you not known? Have you not heard? The Lord is the everlasting God, the Creator of the ends of the earth. He does not faint or grow weary; his understanding is unsearchable. He gives power to the faint, and to him who has no might he increases strength. Even youths shall faint and be weary, and young men shall fall exhausted; but they who wait for the Lord shall renew their strength; they shall mount up with wings like eagles; they shall run and not be weary; they shall walk and not faint.

Exodus 15:2 NKJV
The Lord is my strength and song, and He has become my salvation; He is my God, and I will praise Him; My father's God, and I will exalt Him.

1 Chronicles 16:11 NIV
Look to the Lord and his strength; seek his face always.

1 Peter 5:7 AMPC
Casting the whole of your care [all your anxieties, all your worries, all your concerns, once and for all] on Him, for He cares for you affectionately and cares about you watchfully.

Galatians 6:9-10 NKJV
And let us not grow weary while doing good, for in due season we shall reap if we do not lose heart. Therefore, as we have the opportunity, let us do good to all, especially to those who are of the household of faith.

Nehemiah 8:10 NIV
Do not grieve, for the joy of the Lord is your strength.

Psalm 57:1-3 ESV
Be merciful to me, O God, be merciful to me, for in you my soul takes refuge; in the shadow of your wings I will take refuge, till the storms of destruction pass by. I cry out to God Most High, to God who fulfills his purpose for me. He will send from heaven and save me; he will put to shame him who tramples on me. God will send out his steadfast love and his faithfulness!

Isaiah 41:10 ESV
Fear not, for I am with you; be not dismayed, for I am your God; I will strengthen you, I will help you, I will uphold you with my righteous right hand.

Psalm 18:29-31 AMPC
For by You I can run through a troop, and by my God I can leap over a wall. As for

God, His way is perfect! The word of the Lord is tested and tried; He is a shield to all those who take refuge and put their trust in Him. For who is God except the Lord? Or who is the Rock save our God?

Proverbs 13:12 KJV
Hope deferred maketh the heart sick: but when the desire cometh, it is a tree of life.

Psalm 61:1-4 NKJV
Hear my cry, O God; Attend to my prayer. From the end of the earth I will cry to You, When my heart is overwhelmed; Lead me to the rock that is higher than I. For You have been a shelter for me, A strong tower from the enemy. I will abide in Your tabernacle forever; I will trust in the shelter of Your wings. Selah.

Hebrews 4:16 KJV
Let us therefore come boldly unto the throne of grace, that we may obtain mercy, and find grace to help in time of need.

Matthew 11:28-29 AMPC
Come to Me, all you who labor and are heavy-laden and overburdened, and I will cause you to rest. [I will ease and relieve and refresh your souls]. Take My yoke upon you and learn of Me, for I am gentle (meek) and humble (lowly) in heart, and you will find rest (relief and ease and refreshment and recreation and blessed quiet) for your souls.

Psalm 31:24 AMPC
Be strong and let your heart take courage, all you who wait for and hope for and expect the Lord!

THE LOVE OF GOD

The greatest gift of all is "LOVE". The love of God inspired Him to send His Son to the cross so that we would be redeemed. "But God is so rich in mercy; He loved us so much that even though we were spiritually dead and doomed by our sins, He gave us back our lives again when He raised Christ from the dead..." Ephesians 2:4-5. We abide in God when we abide in His love. Experiencing His perfect love casts out all fear.

1 Peter 4:8 ESV
Above all, keep loving one another earnestly, since love covers a multitude of sins.

1 John 4:7 NKJV
Beloved, let us love one another, for love is of God; and everyone who loves is born of God and knows God.

1 John 4:9 AMPC
In this, the love of God was made manifest (displayed) where we are concerned: in

that God sent His Son, the only begotten or unique [Son], into the world so that we might live through Him.

1 John 4:10 AMPC
In this is love: not that we loved God, but that He loved us and sent His Son to be the propitiation (the atoning sacrifice) for our sins.

1 John 4:11 AMPC
Beloved, if God loved us so [very much], we also ought to love one another.

1 John 4:18 TPT
Love never brings fear, for fear is always related to punishment. But love's perfection drives the fear of punishment far from our hearts. Whoever walks constantly afraid of punishment has not reached love's perfection.

I John 4:19-20 AMPC
We love Him, because He first loved us. If anyone says, I love God, and hates (detests, abominates) his brother [in

Christ], he is a liar; for he who does not love his brother, whom he has seen, cannot love God, whom he has not seen.

John 3:16 AMPC
For God so greatly loved and dearly prized the world that He [even] gave up His only begotten (unique) Son, so that whoever believes in (trusts in, clings to, relies on) Him shall not perish (come to destruction, be lost) but have eternal (everlasting) life.

John 14:23 TPT
Jesus replied, "Loving me empowers you to obey my word. And my Father will love you so deeply that we will come to you and make you our dwelling place."

Psalm 5:11-12 NLT
But let all who take refuge in You rejoice; let them sing joyful praises forever. Spread Your protection over them, that all who love Your name may be filled with joy. For You bless the godly, O Lord; You surround them with Your shield of love.

Ephesians 3:18-19 KJV
May be able to comprehend with all saints what is the breadth, and length, and depth, and height; And to know the love of Christ, which passeth knowledge, that ye might be filled with all the fullness of God.

Romans 8:35, 37-39 NLT
Can anything ever separate us from Christ's love? Does it mean He no longer loves us if we have trouble or calamity, or are persecuted, or hungry, or destitute, or in danger, or threatened with death? No, despite all these things, overwhelming victory is ours through Christ, who loved us. And I am convinced that nothing can ever separate us from God's love. Neither death nor life, neither angels nor demons, neither our fears for today nor our worries about tomorrow — not even the powers of hell can separate us from God's love. No power in the sky above or in the earth below — indeed, nothing in all creation will ever be able to separate us from the love of God that is revealed in Christ Jesus our Lord.

1 Corinthians 13:4-7 NLT
Love is patient and kind. Love is not jealous or boastful or proud or rude. It does not demand its own way. It is not irritable, and it keeps no record of being wronged. It does not rejoice about injustice but rejoices whenever the truth wins out. Love never gives up, never loses faith, is always hopeful, and endures through every circumstance.

Psalm 36:5-7 KJV
Thy mercy, O Lord, is in the heavens; and thy faithfulness reacheth unto the clouds. Thy righteousness is like the great mountains; thy judgments are a great deep: O Lord, thou preservest man and beast. How excellent is thy lovingkindness, O God! Therefore, the children of men put their trust under the shadow of thy wings.

Ephesians 1:5 AMP
He predestined and lovingly planned for us to be adopted to Himself as [His own] children through Jesus Christ, in

accordance with the kind intention and good pleasure of His will.

Romans 5:8 NKJV
But God demonstrates His own love toward us, in that while we were still sinners, Christ died for us.

Ephesians 2:4-7 NKJV
But God, who is rich in mercy, because of His great love with which He loved us, even when we were dead in trespasses, made us alive together with Christ (by grace you have been saved), and raised us up together, and made us sit together in the heavenly places in Christ Jesus, that in the ages to come He might show the exceeding riches of His grace in His kindness toward us in Christ Jesus.

2 Corinthians 5:14-15 AMP
For the love of Christ controls and compels us, because we have concluded this, that One died for all, therefore all died; and He died for all, so that all those who live would

no longer live for themselves, but for Him who died and was raised for their sake.

Romans 5:5 KJV
And hope maketh not ashamed; because the love of God is shed abroad in our hearts by the Holy Ghost, which is given unto us.

Proverbs 3:11-12 NLT
My child, don't reject the Lord's discipline, and don't be upset when He corrects you. For the Lord corrects those He loves, just as a father corrects a child in whom He delights.

Psalm 31:7 NLT
I will be glad and rejoice in Your unfailing love, for You have seen my troubles, and You care about the anguish of my soul.

Lamentations 3:20-23 NLT
I will never forget this awful time, as I grieve over my loss. Yet I still dare to hope when I remember this: The faithful love of the Lord never ends! His mercies never

cease. Great is His faithfulness; His mercies begin afresh each morning.

Lamentations 3:32-33 KJV
But though he causes grief, yet will he have compassion according to the multitude of his mercies. For he doth not afflict willingly nor grieve the children of men.

John 13:3-5, 34 NLT
Jesus knew that the Father had given Him authority over everything and that He had come from God and would return to God. So He got up from the table, took off His robe, wrapped a towel around His waist, and poured water into a basin. Then He began to wash the disciples' feet, drying them with the towel He had around Him. "So now I am giving you a new commandment: Love each other. Just as I have loved you, you should love each other."

Galatians 5:22-23 NLT
But the Holy Spirit produces this kind of fruit in our lives: love, joy, peace,

patience, kindness, goodness, faithfulness, gentleness, and self-control. There is no law against these things!

Hope

Hope: A *feeling of expectation and desire for a certain thing to happen. Like many of the blessings from God in the bible, hope is dynamic and a necessary part in our daily walk with God. Hope is so vital that it is nearly impossible to dream of prosperity, power, greatness, and peace without it.*

1 Peter 1:13 AMP
So prepare your minds for action, be completely sober [in spirit—steadfast, self-disciplined, spiritually and morally alert], fix your hope completely on the grace [of God] that is coming to you when Jesus Christ is revealed.

1 Peter 5:10 AMPC
And after you have suffered a little while, the God of all grace [Who imparts all blessing and favor], Who has called you to His [own] eternal glory in Christ *Jesus*, will Himself complete *and* make you what

you ought to be, establish *and* ground you securely, and strengthen and settle you.

Proverbs 13:12 AMP
Hope deferred makes the heart sick,
But when desire is fulfilled, it is a tree of life.

1 Thessalonians 1:3 KJV
Remembering without ceasing your work of faith, and labour of love, and patience of hope in our Lord Jesus Christ, in the sight of God and our Father.

Ephesians 1:18 AMP
And [I pray] that the eyes of your heart [the very center and core of your being] may be enlightened [flooded with light by the Holy Spirit], so that you will know *and* cherish the [a]hope [the divine guarantee, the confident expectation] to which He has called you, the riches of His glorious inheritance in the saints (God's people).

Hebrews 10:23 NKJV
Let us hold fast the confession of our hope without wavering, for He who promised is faithful.

Hebrews 10:23 AMPC
So let us seize and hold fast and retain without wavering the hope we cherish, and confess and our acknowledgement of it, for He Who promised is reliable (sure) and faithful to His word.

Isaiah 40:31 AMPC
But those who hope in the Lord will renew their strength. They will soar on wings like eagles; they will run and not grow weary, they will walk and not be faint.

Romans 15:13 ESV
May the God of hope fill you with all joy and peace in believing, so that by the power of the Holy Spirit you may abound in hope.

Romans 12:12 ESV
Rejoice in hope, be patient in tribulation, be constant in prayer.

Jeremiah 29:11 AMP
For I know the plans *and* thoughts that I have for you,' says the Lord, 'plans for peace *and* well-being and not for disaster, to give you a future and a hope.

Psalm 42:11 NKJ
Why are you cast down, O my soul? And why are you disquieted within me? Hope in God; For I shall yet praise Him, the help of my countenance and my God.

Hebrews 6:19 AMP
This hope [this confident assurance] we have as an anchor of the soul [it cannot slip and it cannot break down under whatever pressure bears upon it]—a safe and steadfast hope that enters within the veil [of the heavenly temple, that most Holy Place in which the very presence of God dwells].

Romans 5:3-5 KJV
And not only so, but we glory in tribulations also: knowing that tribulation worketh patience; And patience, experience; and experience, hope: And hope maketh not ashamed; because the love of God is shed abroad in our hearts by the Holy Ghost which is given unto us.

1 Corinthians 13:13 KJV
And now abideth faith, hope, charity, these three; but the greatest of these is charity.

1 Peter 1:3-5 ESV
Blessed be the God and Father of our Lord Jesus Christ! According to his great mercy, he has caused us to be born again to a living hope through the resurrection of Jesus Christ from the dead, to an inheritance that is imperishable, undefiled, and unfading, kept in heaven for you, who by God's power are being guarded through faith for a salvation ready to be revealed in the last time.

God's Guidance and Direction

Created for a purpose, yet has not been attainable? Promises spoken yet not seen. So, how do you get there? No one wants to walk in the wrong direction and miss their God-given purpose, goals, and/or desires. The Word of God says, "I will bring the blind by a way they did not know; I will lead them in paths they have not known. I will make darkness light before them, and crooked places straight. These things I will do for them, and not forsake them" (Isaiah 42:16). He is ordering your steps by His Word through the Person of the Holy Spirit.

Ephesians 5:15-17 ESV
Look carefully at how you walk, not as unwise but as wise, making the best use of the time, because the days are evil. Therefore, do not be foolish, but understand what the will of the Lord is.

Psalm 5:8 NLT
Lead me in the right path, O Lord, or my enemies will conquer me. Make your way plain for me to follow.

Psalm 119:105 NLT
Your word is a lamp to guide my feet and a light for my path.

Proverbs 12:26 AMP
The righteous man is a guide to his neighbor, but the way of the wicked leads them astray.

John 16:13 KJV
Howbeit when he, the Spirit of truth, is come, he will guide you into all truth: for he shall not speak of himself; but whatsoever he shall hear, that shall he speak: and he will shew you things to come.

Psalm 25:9 ESV
He leads the humble in what is right, and teaches the humble his way.

Psalm 32:8 KJV
I will instruct thee and teach thee in the way which thou shalt go: I will guide thee with mine eye.

Psalm 23:3 KJV
He restoreth my soul: he leadeth me in the paths of righteousness for his name's sake.

Jeremiah 3:15 KJV
And I will give you pastors according to mine heart, which shall feed you with knowledge and understanding.

Isaiah 42:16 NKJV
I will bring the blind by a way they did not know; I will lead them in paths they have not known. I will make darkness light before them, and crooked places straight; these things I will do for them, and not forsake them.

Psalm 73:24 NKJV
You will guide me with Your counsel,
And afterward receive me to glory.

Psalm 48:14 ESV
That this is God, our God forever and ever. He will guide us forever.

Exodus 15:13 NKJV
You, in Your mercy [*love*], have led forth the people whom You have redeemed; You have guided them in Your strength to Your holy habitation.

Isaiah 30:21 NKJV
Your ears shall hear a word behind you, saying, "This is the way, walk in it, "Whenever you turn to the right hand or whenever you turn to the left.

Isaiah 58:11 NLT
The Lord will guide you continually, giving you water when you are dry and restoring your strength. You will be like a well-watered garden, like an ever-flowing spring.

Proverbs 3:5-6 AMP
Trust in and rely confidently on the Lord with all your heart, and do not rely on your

own insight or understanding. In all your ways know and acknowledge and recognize Him, and He will make your paths straight and smooth [removing obstacles that block your way].

John 8:12 NKJV
Then Jesus spoke to them again, saying, "I am the light of the world. He who follows Me shall not walk in darkness, but have the light of life."

Galatians 5:25 NKJV
If we live in the Spirit, let us also walk in the Spirit.

1 Corinthians 2:12 NLT
And we have received God's Spirit (not the world's spirit), so we can know the wonderful things God has freely given us.

Luke 4:1 NLT
Then Jesus, full of the Holy Spirit, returned from the Jordan River. He was led by the Spirit in the wilderness.

Romans 6:18 KJV
Being then made free from sin, ye became the servants of righteousness.

Psalm 139:9 NKJV
If I take the wings of the morning *and* dwell in the uttermost parts of the sea, even there Your hand shall lead me, and Your right hand shall hold me.

Romans 6:16 NLT
Don't you realize that you become the slave of whatever you choose to obey? You can be a slave to sin, which leads to death, or you can choose to obey God, which leads to righteous living.

1 Corinthians 2:10 KJV
But God hath revealed them unto us by his Spirit: for the Spirit searcheth all things, yea, the deep things of God.

Psalm 37:23-24 KJV
The steps of a good man are ordered by the Lord: and he delighteth in his way. Though he fall, he shall not be utterly

cast down: for the Lord upholdeth him with his hand.

Jeremiah 33:3 KJV
Call unto me, and I will answer thee, and show thee great and mighty things, which thou knowest not.

Proverbs 14:12 KJV
There is a way which seemeth right unto a man, but the end thereof are the ways of death.

SURRENDERING TO GOD

Surrendering to God means that you yield and relinquish your possessions, your way, and your very being to Him. It is denying yourself as you totally allow Christ to be the Lord of your life, and that you are willing to put absolute trust in God completely. Surrendering means admitting you are powerless and need help.

Matthew 16:23-26 ESV
Then Jesus told his disciples, "If anyone would come after me, let him deny himself and take up his cross and follow me. For whoever would save his life will lose it, but whoever loses his life for my sake will find it. For what will it profit a man if he gains the whole world and forfeits his soul? Or what shall a man give in return for his soul?"

James 4:7 ESV
Submit yourselves therefore to God. Resist the devil, and he will flee from you.

Matthew 7:7 ESV
Ask, and it will be given to you; seek, and you will find; knock, and it will be opened to you.

Romans 6:23 ESV
For the wages of sin is death, but the free gift of God is eternal life in Christ Jesus our Lord.

Luke 9:23 ESV
And he said to all, "If anyone would come after me, let him deny himself and take up his cross daily and follow me.

Romans 8:29 ESV
For those whom he foreknew, he also predestined to be conformed to the image of his Son, in order that he might be the firstborn among many brothers.

John 6:44 ESV
No one can come to me unless the Father who sent me draws him. And I will raise him up on the last day.

Ezekiel 18:4 ESV
Behold, all souls are mine; the soul of the father as well as the soul of the son is mine: the soul who sins shall die.

John 17:17 ESV
Sanctify them in the truth; your word is truth.

Philippians 2:13 ESV
For it is God who works in you, both to will and to work for his good pleasure.

Romans 12:2 KJV
And be not conformed to this world: but be ye transformed by the renewing of your mind, that ye may prove what is that good, and acceptable, and perfect, will of God.

James 4:10 KJV
Humble yourselves in the sight of the Lord, and he shall lift you up.

Luke 9:23 NKJV
Then He said to them all, "If anyone desires to come after Me, let him deny

himself, and take up his cross daily, and follow Me.

Matthew 11:28-29 NKJV
Come to Me, all you who labor and are heavy laden, and I will give you rest. Take My yoke upon you and learn from Me, for I am gentle and lowly in heart, and you will find rest for your souls.

James 4:7 AMP
So submit to [the authority of] God. Resist the devil [stand firm against him] and he will flee from you.

FINANCES

The Lord wants to speak to you through His Word to encourage you, build your faith, and let you know that He is right there to walk with you through whatever you are facing financially. "The silver is Mine, and the gold is Mine,' declares the Lord of hosts." Haggai 2:8

Psalm 32:8 KJV
I will instruct thee and teach thee in the way which thou shalt go: I will guide thee with mine eye.

Deuteronomy 31:8 NLT
The Lord himself goes before you and will be with you; he will never leave you nor forsake you. Do not be afraid; do not be discouraged."

Jeremiah 29:11 NIV
For I know the plans I have for you," declares the Lord, "plans to prosper you and not to harm you, plans to give you hope and a future.

Psalm 35:27 NKJV

Let them shout for joy and be glad, who favor my righteous cause; And let them say continually, "Let the Lord be magnified, who has pleasure in the prosperity of His servant."

Proverb 10:22 KJV

The blessing of the Lord, it maketh rich, and he addeth no sorrow with it.

Proverb 3:9-10 NKJV

Honor the Lord with your possessions,
And with the first fruits of all your increase;
So your barns will be filled with plenty, and your vats will overflow with new wine.

Isaiah 45:2-3 NKJV

I will go before you and make the crooked places straight; I will break in pieces the gates of bronze and cut the bars of iron. I will give you the treasures of darkness and hidden riches of secret places, that you may know that I, the Lord, who calls you by your name, am the God of Israel.

Deuteronomy 8:18 AMP
But you shall remember [with profound respect] the Lord your God, for it is He who is giving you power to make wealth, that He may confirm His covenant which He swore (solemnly promised) to your fathers, as it is this day.

Luke 6:38 NKJV
Give, and it will be given to you: good measure, pressed down, shaken together, and running over will be put into your bosom. For with the same measure that you use, it will be measured back to you.

Psalm 84:10-12 NLT
A single day in your courts is better than a thousand anywhere else! I would rather be a gatekeeper in the house of my God than live the good life in the homes of the wicked. For the Lord God is our sun and our shield. He gives us grace and glory.
The Lord will withhold no good thing
from those who do what is right.
O Lord of Heaven's armies, what
joy for those who trust in you.

2 Corinthians 9:6-8 ESV
The point is this: whoever sows sparingly will also reap sparingly, and whoever sows bountifully will also reap bountifully. Each one must give as he has decided in his heart, not reluctantly or under compulsion, for God loves a cheerful giver. And God is able to make all grace abound to you, so that having all sufficiency in all things at all times, you may abound in every good work.

Philippians 4:19 NLT
And this same God who takes care of me will supply all your needs from his glorious riches, which have been given to us in Christ Jesus.

PROTECTION AND SAFETY

Throughout the Bible, God has been our Defense, our Fortress, our Hightower. He is our Rock and our Refuge in times of trouble. El Roi, "the God Who sees me," has given His angels charge over us to keep us in all our ways. Psalm 139:5, "You have hedged me behind and before, And laid Your hand upon me." So abide under the shadow of the Almighty God, El Shaddai!.

Psalm 56:9 KJV
When I cry unto thee, then shall mine enemies turn back: this I know; for God is for me.

Psalm 9:9-10 GWT
You, Lord, are a stronghold for the oppressed, a stronghold in times of trouble. Those who know Your name trust You, O Lord, because You have never deserted those who seek Your help.

Psalm 16:1 NIV
Keep me safe, my God, for in You I take refuge.

Psalm 17:8 AMP
Keep me [in Your affectionate care, protect me] as the apple of Your eye; Hide me in the [protective] shadow of Your wings.

Psalm 23:4 NIV
Even though I walk through the darkest valley, I will fear no evil, for You are with me; Your rod and Your staff, they comfort me.

Psalm 32:7 NIV
You are my hiding place; You will protect me from trouble and surround me with songs of deliverance.

Psalm 57:1 NIV
Have mercy on me, O God, have mercy, for in You my soul takes refuge. I will take refuge in the shadow of Your wing until the danger has passed.

Psalm 121:5-8 ESV
The Lord is your keeper; the Lord is your shade on your right hand. The sun shall not strike you by day, nor the moon by night. The Lord will keep you from all evil; he will keep your life. The Lord will keep your going out and your coming in from this time forth and forevermore.

Psalm 91:1-7 TPT
When you abide under the shadow of Shaddai, you are hidden in the strength of God Most High. He's the hope that holds me and the stronghold to shelter me, the only God for me, and my great confidence. He will rescue you from every hidden trap of the enemy, and he will protect you from false accusation and any deadly curse. His massive arms are wrapped around you, protecting you. You can run under his covering of majesty and hide. His arms of faithfulness are a shield keeping you from harm. You will never worry about an attack of demonic forces at night, nor have to fear a spirit of darkness coming against you. Don't fear a thing! Whether by night

or by day, demonic danger will not trouble you, nor will the powers of evil be launched against you. Even in a time of disaster, with thousands and thousands being killed, you will remain unscathed and unharmed.

Matthew 6:13 ESV
Lead us not into temptation, but deliver us from evil.

Romans 8:31, 37-39 NIV
If God is for us, who can be against us? We are more than conquerors through him who loved us. For I am convinced that neither death nor life, neither angels nor demons, neither the present nor the future, nor any powers, neither height nor depth, nor anything else in all creation, will be able to separate us from the love of God that is in Christ Jesus our Lord.

1 Corinthians 10:13
No temptation has overtaken you except what is common to mankind. And God is faithful; he will not let you be tempted beyond what you can bear. But when you

are tempted, he will also provide a way out so that you can endure it.

2 Thessalonians 3:3 NIV
But the Lord is faithful, and he will strengthen you and protect you from the evil one.

Deuteronomy 31:6 NKJV
Be strong and of good courage, do not fear nor be afraid of them; for the Lord your God, He is the One who goes with you. He will not leave you nor forsake you.

Isaiah 41:10 NIV
So do not fear, for I am with you; do not be dismayed, for I am your God. I will strengthen you and help you; I will uphold you with my righteous right hand.

Proverbs 2:11 NIV
Discretion will protect you, and understanding will guard you.

Proverbs 4:6 NIV
Do not forsake wisdom, and she will protect you; love her, and she will watch over you.

THE ANOINTING

It is the Anointing that destroys the yokes of bondage

1 John 2:27 NKJV
But the anointing which you have received from Him abides in you, and you do not need that anyone teach you; but as the same anointing teaches you concerning all things, and is true, and is not a lie, and just as it has taught you, you will abide in Him.

1 John 2:20 NKJV
But you have an anointing from the Holy One, and you know all things.

Luke 4:18-19 ESV
The Spirit of the Lord is upon me, because he has anointed me to proclaim good news to the poor. He has sent me to proclaim liberty to the captives and recovering of sight to the blind, to set at liberty those who are oppressed, to proclaim the year of the Lord's favor.

James 5:14 ESV
Is anyone among you sick? Let him call for the elders of the church, and let them pray over him, anointing him with oil in the name of the Lord.

2 Corinthians 1:21-22 ESV
And it is God who establishes us with you in Christ, and has anointed us, and who has also put his seal on us and given us his Spirit in our hearts as a guarantee.

Hebrews 1:9 NKJV
You have loved righteousness and hated wickedness; therefore God, your God, has anointed you with the oil of gladness beyond your companions.

Isaiah 61:1-3 NKJV
"The Spirit of the Lord God is upon Me, Because the Lord has anointed Me to preach good tidings to the poor; He has sent Me to heal the brokenhearted, To proclaim liberty to the captives, And the opening of the prison to those who are bound; To proclaim the acceptable year of

the Lord, And the day of vengeance of our God; To comfort all who mourn, To console those who mourn in Zion, To give them beauty for ashes, The oil of joy for mourning, The garment of praise for the spirit of heaviness; they may be called trees of righteousness, the planting of the Lord, that He may be glorified."

Isaiah 10:27 KJV
And it shall come to pass in that day, that his burden shall be taken away from off thy shoulder, and his yoke from off thy neck, and the yoke shall be destroyed because of the anointing.

Acts 10:30 KJV
How God anointed Jesus of Nazareth with the Holy Ghost and with power: who went about doing good, and healing all that were oppressed of the devil; for God was with him.

1 Thessalonians 1:5 KJV
For our gospel came not unto you in word only, but also in power, and in the Holy

Ghost, and in much assurance; as ye know what manner of men we were among you for your sake.

Joel 2:28-29 NKJV

"And it shall come to pass afterward that I will pour out My Spirit on all flesh;
Your sons and your daughters shall prophesy, Your old men shall dream dreams, Your young men shall see visions.
And also on My menservants and on My maidservants I will pour out My Spirit in those days."

Psalm 45:7 KJV

Thou lovest righteousness, and hatest wickedness: therefore God, thy God, hath anointed thee with the oil of gladness above thy fellows.

Psalm 105:15 KJV

Saying, Touch not mine anointed, and do my prophets no harm.

Mark 6:13 ESV
And they cast out many demons and anointed with oil many who were sick and healed them.

Psalm 23:4-6 ESV
Even though I walk through the valley of the shadow of death, I will fear no evil, for you are with me; your rod and your staff, they comfort me. You prepare a table before me in the presence of my enemies; you anoint my head with oil; my cup overflows. Surely goodness and mercy shall follow me all the days of my life, and I shall dwell in the house of the Lord forever.

Psalm 28:7-8 ESV
The Lord is my strength and my shield; in him my heart trusts, and I am helped; my heart exults, and with my song I give thanks to him. The Lord is the strength of his people; he is the saving refuge of his anointed.

Acts 10:37-38 KJV
That word, I say, ye know, which was published throughout all Judaea, and began from Galilee, after the baptism which John preached; How God anointed Jesus of Nazareth with the Holy Ghost and with power: who went about doing good, and healing all that were oppressed of the devil; for God was with him.

Psalm 20:6-7 AMP
Now I know that the Lord saves His anointed; He will answer him from His holy heaven With the saving strength of His right hand. Some trust in chariots and some in horses, but we will remember and trust in the name of the Lord our God.

WALKING IN SPIRITUAL AUTHORITY

Spiritual authority is defined as the right to make use of God's power to enforce spiritual law, which is literally the Word of God. We have a responsibility to walk in this authority.

Luke 10:19 ESV
Behold, I have given you authority to tread on serpents and scorpions, and over all the power of the enemy, and nothing shall hurt you.

Luke 9:1 ESV
And he called the twelve together and gave them power and authority over all demons and to cure diseases.

Romans 13:1 ESV
Let every person be subject to the governing authorities. For there is no authority except from God, and those that exist have been instituted by God.

Matthew 28:18 ESV
And Jesus came and said to them, "All authority in heaven and on earth has been given to me."

James 4:7 ESV
Submit yourselves therefore to God. Resist the devil, and he will flee from you.

Hebrews 13:17 ESV
Obey your leaders and submit to them, for they are keeping watch over your souls, as those who will have to give an account. Let them do this with joy and not with groaning, for that would be of no advantage to you.

Matthew 18:18-20 ESV
Truly, I say to you, whatever you bind on earth shall be bound in heaven, and whatever you loose on earth shall be loosed in heaven. Again I say to you, if two of you agree on earth about anything they ask, it will be done for them by my Father in heaven. For where two or three

are gathered in my name, there am I among them."

1 John 4:4 NKJV
You are of God, little children, and have overcome them, because He who is in you is greater than he who is in the world.

Matthew 16:15-19 ESV
He said to them, "But who do you say that I am?" Simon Peter replied, "You are the Christ, the Son of the living God." And Jesus answered him, "Blessed are you, Simon Bar-Jonah! For flesh and blood has not revealed this to you, but my Father who is in heaven. And I tell you, you are Peter, and on this rock I will build my church, and the gates of hell shall not prevail against it. I will give you the keys of the kingdom of heaven, and whatever you bind on earth shall be bound in heaven, and whatever you loose on earth shall be loosed in heaven."

2 Corinthians 10:3-5 ESV
For though we walk in the flesh, we are not waging war according to the flesh. For the weapons of our warfare are not of the flesh but have divine power to destroy strongholds. We destroy arguments and every lofty opinion raised against the knowledge of God, and take every thought captive to obey Christ.

Mark 16:17-18 ESV
And these signs will accompany those who believe: in my name they will cast out demons; they will speak in new tongues; they will pick up serpents with their hands; and if they drink any deadly poison, it will not hurt them; they will lay their hands on the sick, and they will recover."

John 10:27 ESV
My sheep hear my voice, and I know them, and they follow me.

1 John 5:4-5 NKJV
For whatever is born of God overcomes the world. And this is the victory that has overcome the world—our faith. Who is he who overcomes the world, but he who believes that Jesus is the Son of God?

Deuteronomy 28:7 ESV
The Lord will cause your enemies who rise against you to be defeated before you. They shall come out against you one way and flee before you seven ways.

1 John 3:8 ESV
Whoever makes a practice of sinning is of the devil, for the devil has been sinning from the beginning. The reason the Son of God appeared was to destroy the works of the devil.

Genesis 1:28 ESV
And God blessed them. And God said to them, "Be fruitful and multiply and fill the earth and subdue it and have dominion over the fish of the sea and over the birds

of the heavens and over every living thing that moves on the earth."

Romans 12:1-5 ESV
I appeal to you, therefore, brothers, by the mercies of God, to present your bodies as a living sacrifice, holy and acceptable to God, which is your spiritual worship. Do not be conformed to this world, but be transformed by the renewal of your mind, that by testing you may discern what is the will of God, what is good and acceptable and perfect. For by the grace given to me I say to everyone among you not to think of himself more highly than he ought to think, but to think with sober judgment, each according to the measure of faith that God has assigned. For as in one body we have many members, and the members do not all have the same function, so we, though many, are one body in Christ, and individually members one of another.

John 16:13 ESV
When the Spirit of truth comes, he will guide you into all the truth, for he will not speak on his own authority, but whatever he hears he will speak, and he will declare to you the things that are to come.

2 Corinthians 10:4 ESV
For the weapons of our warfare are not of the flesh but have divine power to destroy strongholds.

Acts 20:28 ESV
Pay careful attention to yourselves and to all the flock, in which the Holy Spirit has made you overseers, to care for the church of God, which he obtained with his own blood.

Hebrews 4:12-13 ESV
For the word of God is living and active, sharper than any two-edged sword, piercing to the division of soul and of spirit, of joints and of marrow, and discerning the thoughts and intentions

of the heart. And no creature is hidden from his sight, but all are naked and exposed to the eyes of him to whom we must give an account.

Philippians 2:9-11 ESV
Therefore God has highly exalted him and bestowed on him the name that is above every name, so that at the name of Jesus every knee should bow, in heaven and on earth, and under the earth, and every tongue confess that Jesus Christ is Lord, to the glory of God the Father.

Ephesians 6:10-20 ESV
Finally, be strong in the Lord and in the strength of his might. Put on the whole armor of God, that you may be able to stand against the schemes of the devil. For we do not wrestle against flesh and blood, but against the rulers, against the authorities, against the cosmic powers over this present darkness, against the spiritual forces of evil in the heavenly places. Therefore, take up the whole

armor of God, that you may be able to withstand in the evil day, and having done all, to stand firm. Stand therefore, having fastened on the belt of truth, and having put on the breastplate of righteousness, and, as shoes for your feet, having put on the readiness given by the gospel of peace. In all circumstances, take up the shield of faith, with which you can extinguish all the flaming darts of the evil one; and take the helmet of salvation, and the sword of the Spirit, which is the word of God, praying at all times in the Spirit, with all prayer and supplication. To that end, keep alert with all perseverance, making supplication for all the saints, and also for me, that words may be given to me in opening my mouth boldly to proclaim the mystery of the gospel, for which I am an ambassador in chains, that I may declare it boldly, as I ought to speak.

2 Corinthians 10:5 ESV
We destroy arguments and every lofty opinion raised against the knowledge of

God, and take every thought captive to obey Christ.

1 Peter 5:8 ESV
Be sober-minded; be watchful. Your adversary, the devil, prowls around like a roaring lion, seeking someone to devour.

Mark 16:20 NKJV
And they went out and preached everywhere, the Lord working with them and confirming the word through the accompanying signs. Amen.

THE NATIONAL LEADERS

Being a leader takes courage, discipline, and determination. Every leader is accountable to God for their actions. God ordained and placed each leader in their position for His purpose and His glory.

Psalm 2:10-11 NIV
Therefore, you kings, be wise; be warned, you rulers of the earth. Serve the Lord with fear and celebrate his rule with trembling.

Proverbs 11:14 NIV
For lack of guidance, a nation falls, but victory is won through many advisers.

Daniel 2:21-22 NKVJ
And He changes the times and the seasons; He removes kings and raises up kings; He gives wisdom to the wise And knowledge to those who have understanding. He reveals deep and secret things; He knows what is in the darkness, and light dwells with Him.

Proverbs 21:1 KJV
The king's heart is in the hand of the Lord, as the rivers of water: he turneth it whithersoever he will.

Proverbs 2:1-8 NIV
My son, if you accept my words and store up my commands within you, turning your ear to wisdom and applying your heart to understanding-indeed, if you call out for insight and cry aloud for understanding, and if you look for it as for silver and search for it as for hidden treasure, then you will understand the fear of the Lord and find the knowledge of God. For the Lord gives wisdom; from his mouth comes knowledge and understanding. He holds success in store for the upright; he is a shield to those whose walk is blameless, for he guards the course of the just and protects the way of his faithful ones.

2 Chronicles 7:14 NIV
If my people, who are called by my name, will humble themselves and pray and seek my face and turn from their wicked ways,

then I will hear from heaven, and I will forgive their sin and will heal their land.

Hebrews 13:7 NIV
Remember your leaders, who spoke the word of God to you. Consider the outcome of their way of life and imitate their faith.

Isaiah 41:10 NIV
So do not fear, for I am with you; do not be dismayed, for I am your God. I will strengthen you and help you; I will uphold you with my righteous right hand.

James 1:12 NIV
Blessed is the one who perseveres under trial because, having stood the test, that person will receive the crown of life that the Lord has promised to those who love him.

1 Timothy 2:1-2 NIV
I urge, then, first of all, that petitions, prayers, intercession, and thanksgiving be made for all people-for kings and all those

in authority, that we may live peaceful and quiet lives in all godliness and holiness.

Daniel 4:17 TLB
For this has been decreed by the Watchers, demanded by the Holy Ones. The purpose of this decree is that all the world may understand that the Most High dominates the kingdoms of the world and gives them to anyone he wants to, even the lowliest of men!

Romans 13:1 NIV
Let everyone be subject to the governing authorities, for there is no authority except that which God has established. The authorities that exist have been established by God.

Job 12:23-25 NKJV
He makes nations great, and destroys them; He enlarges nations, and guides them. He takes away the understanding of the chiefs of the people of the earth, and makes them wander in a pathless wilderness. They grope in the dark

without light, and He makes them stagger like a drunken man.

Matthew 20:26 NKJV
Yet it shall not be so among you; but whoever desires to become great among you, let him be your servant.

Luke 12:48 TLB
But anyone who is not aware that he is doing wrong will be punished only lightly. Much is required from those to whom much is given, for their responsibility is greater.

Acts 20:28 AMP
Be on guard for yourselves and for all the flock, among which the Holy Spirit has made you overseers, to shepherd the church of God, which He purchased with His own blood.

1 Timothy 3:5 AMP
But if a man does not know how to manage his own household, how will he take care of the church of God?

Proverbs 29:2 AMP
When the righteous increase, the people rejoice, but when a wicked man rules, people groan.

Proverbs 31: 8-9 AMP
Speak up for those who cannot speak for themselves, for the rights of all who are destitute. Speak up and judge fairly; defend the rights of the poor and needy.

Daniel 2:37-38 TLB
Your Majesty, you are a king over many kings, for the God of heaven has given you your kingdom, power, strength, and glory. You rule the farthest provinces, and even animals and birds are under your control, as God decreed. You are that head of gold.

DISTRACTIONS AND PROCRASTINATION

- *"The more you focus on yourself, the more distracted you will be from the proper path. The more you know God and commune with Him, the more the Spirit will make you like Him. The more you are like Him, the better you will understand His utter sufficiency for all of life's difficulties. And that is the only way to know real satisfaction." -John MacArthur*
- *"God did not create you to live a distracted life. God created you to live a Jesus-infused life."*
- *"Don't let the noise of the world keep you from hearing the voice of the Lord."*
- *"If the enemy can't destroy you, he will distract you."*

1 Corinthians 7:35 NKJV
And this I say for your own profit, not that I may put a leash on you, but for what is proper, and that you may serve the Lord without distraction.

Romans 12:2 ESV
Do not be conformed to this world, but be transformed by the renewal of your mind, that by testing you may discern what is the will of God, what is good and acceptable and perfect.

1 John 2:15 NKJV
Do not love the world or the things in the world. If anyone loves the world, the love of the Father is not in him.

Hebrews 12:2 ISV
Fixing our attention on Jesus, the pioneer and perfecter of the faith, who, in view of the joy set before him, endured the cross, disregarding its shame, and has sat down at the right hand of the throne of God.

1 Peter 5:8 KJV
Be sober, be vigilant; because your adversary the devil, as a roaring lion, walketh about, seeking whom he may devour.

Mark 1:35 KJV
And in the morning, rising up a great while before day, he went out, and departed into a solitary place, and there prayed.

Hebrews 12:2 AMP
[looking away from all that will distract us and] focusing our eyes on Jesus, who is the Author and Perfecter of faith [the first incentive for our belief and the One who brings our faith to maturity], who for the joy [of accomplishing the goal] set before Him endured the cross, disregarding the shame, and sat down at the right hand of the throne of God [revealing His deity, His authority, and the completion of His work].

Colossians 3:1-2 KJV
If ye then be risen with Christ, seek those things which are above, where Christ sitteth on the right hand of God. Set your affection on things above, not on things on the earth.

Proverbs 4:25 NLT
Look straight ahead, and fix your eyes on what lies before you.

Mark 4:19 AMP
But the worries and cares of the world [the distractions of this age with its worldly pleasures], and the deceitfulness [and the false security or glamour] of wealth [or fame], and the passionate desires for all the other things creep in and choke out the word, and it becomes unfruitful.

Psalm 119:15 TPT
I set my heart on your precepts and pay close attention to all your ways.

The Mercy of God

Our God is rich in mercy. Mercy is a willingness to forgive an offender or adversary. Also, it can be the ability to spare or help another. Mercy has been defined as God not giving us what we deserve. God's greatest demonstration of His mercy for mankind was displayed by His Son's innocent death on the cross. Though He knew no sin, He became sin on our behalf, delivering us from eternal destruction. Still, even to this day, His mercy continues, for if we confess our sins, He is faithful and just to forgive us of our sins and cleanse us of all unrighteousness. (See I John 1:9)

Hebrews 4:16 ESV
Let us then with confidence draw near to the throne of grace, that we may receive mercy and find grace to help in time of need.

James 2:13 ESV
For judgment is without mercy to one who has shown no mercy. Mercy triumphs over judgment.

Psalm 86:5 ESV
For you, O Lord, are good and forgiving, abounding in steadfast love to all who call upon you.

Luke 6:36 ESV
Be merciful, even as your Father is merciful.

Micah 6:8 ESV
He has told you, O man, what is good; and what does the Lord require of you but to do justice, and to love kindness, and to walk humbly with your God?

1 John 1:9 ESV
If we confess our sins, he is faithful and just to forgive us our sins and to cleanse us from all unrighteousness.

1 Peter 1:3 ESV
Blessed be the God and Father of our Lord Jesus Christ! According to his great mercy, he has caused us to be born again to a living hope through the resurrection of Jesus Christ from the dead.

1 Timothy 1:16 ESV
But I received mercy for this reason, that in me, as the foremost, Jesus Christ might display his perfect patience as an example to those who were to believe in him for eternal life.

2 Peter 3:9 ESV
The Lord is not slow to fulfill his promise as some count slowness, but is patient toward you, not wishing that any should perish, but that all should reach repentance.

2 Samuel 22:26 ESV
With the merciful you show yourself merciful; with the blameless man you show yourself blameless.

Ephesians 2:4 ESV
But God, being rich in mercy, because of the great love with which he loved us.

Exodus 34:6 ESV
The Lord passed before him and proclaimed, "The Lord, the Lord, a God merciful and gracious, slow to anger, and abounding in steadfast love and faithfulness."

John 3:16 ESV
For God so loved the world, that he gave his only Son, that whoever believes in him should not perish but have eternal life.

Proverbs 28:13 ESV
Whoever conceals his transgressions will not prosper, but he who confesses and forsakes them will obtain mercy.

Matthew 5:7 ESV
Blessed are the merciful, for they shall receive mercy.

Matthew 9:13 ESV
"Go and learn what this means, 'I desire mercy, and not sacrifice.' For I came not to call the righteous, but sinners."

Micah 7:18 ESV
Who is a God like you, pardoning iniquity and passing over transgression for the remnant of his inheritance? He does not retain his anger forever, because he delights in steadfast love.

Romans 9:18 ESV
So then he has mercy on whomever he wills, and he hardens whomever he wills.

Titus 3:5 ESV
He saved us, not because of works done by us in righteousness, but according to his own mercy, by the washing of regeneration and renewal of the Holy Spirit.

Psalm 103:8-10 KJV
The Lord is merciful and gracious, slow to anger, and plenteous in mercy. He will not always chide: neither will he keep his anger

forever. He hath not dealt with us after our sins; nor rewarded us according to our iniquities.

Psalm 145:8 KJV
The Lord is gracious, and full of compassion; slow to anger, and of great mercy.

THE GRACE OF GOD

Grace, "charis" as defined in the New Testament, is a benefit bestowed to show kindness or favor. Grace is God giving us what we don't deserve: eternal life. Ephesians 2:8-9, "For by grace are ye saved through faith; and that not of yourselves: it is the gift of God: Not of works, lest any man should boast."

2 Corinthians 12:9 KJV
And he said unto me, My grace is sufficient for thee: for my strength is made perfect in weakness. Most gladly, therefore, will I rather glory in my infirmities, that the power of Christ may rest upon me.

1 Peter 5:10 KJV
But the God of all grace, who hath called us unto his eternal glory by Christ Jesus, after that ye have suffered a while, make you perfect, stablish, strengthen, settle you.

Titus 2:11 AMP
For the [remarkable, undeserved] grace of God that brings salvation has appeared to all men.

Romans 3:23-24 NLT
For everyone has sinned; we all fall short of God's glorious standard. Yet God, in his grace, freely makes us right in his sight. He did this through Christ Jesus when He freed us from the penalty for our sins.

Ephesians 2:4-6 NLT
But God is so rich in mercy, and he loved us so much that even though we were dead because of our sins, he gave us life when he raised Christ from the dead. (It is only by God's grace that you have been saved!) For he raised us from the dead along with Christ and seated us with him in the heavenly realms because we are united with Christ Jesus.

John 1:17 NLT
For the law was given by Moses, but grace and truth came by Jesus Christ.

Romans 11:6 KJV
And if by grace, then is it no more of works: otherwise grace is no more grace. But if it be of works, then is it no more grace: otherwise work is no more work.

Romans 5:2 KJV
By whom also we have access by faith into this grace wherein we stand, and rejoice in hope of the glory of God.

Titus 3:7 AMP
So that we would be justified [made free of the guilt of sin] by His [compassionate, undeserved] grace, and that we would be [acknowledged as acceptable to Him and] made heirs of eternal life [actually experiencing it] according to our hope (His guarantee).

Ephesians 1:7-12 NKJV

In Him we have redemption through his blood, the forgiveness of sins, according to the riches of His grace, which He made to abound toward us in all wisdom and prudence, having made known to us the mystery of His will, according to His good pleasure which He purposed in Himself, that in the dispensation of the fullness of the times He might gather together in one all things in Christ, both which are in heaven and which are on earth—in Him. In Him also we have obtained an inheritance, being predestined according to the purpose of Him who works all things according to the counsel of His will, that we who first trusted in Christ should be to the praise of His glory.

2 Timothy 1:9 NLT

For God saved us and called us to live a holy life. He did this, not because we deserved it, but because that was his plan from before the beginning of time—to show us his grace through Christ Jesus.

2 Corinthians 9:8 NKJV
And God is able to make all grace abound toward you, that you, always having all sufficiency in all things, may have an abundance for every good work.

Titus 3:5 KJV
Not by works of righteousness which we have done, but according to his mercy he saved us, by the washing of regeneration, and renewing of the Holy Ghost.

Hebrews 4:16 ESV
Let us then with confidence draw near to the throne of grace, that we may receive mercy and find grace to help in time of need.

Ephesians 2:8 ESV
For by grace you have been saved through faith. And this is not your own doing; it is the gift of God.

James 4:6 ESV
But he gives more grace. Therefore, it says, "God opposes the proud, but gives grace to the humble."

1 Corinthians 15:10 ESV
But by the grace of God I am what I am, and his grace toward me was not in vain. On the contrary, I worked harder than any of them, though it was not I, but the grace of God that is with me.

1 Peter 4:10 KJV
As every man hath received the gift, even so minister the same one to another, as good stewards of the manifold grace of God.

2 Timothy 2:1 ESV
You then, my child, be strengthened by the grace that is in Christ Jesus.

Romans 5:20-21 ESV
Now the law came in to increase the trespass, but where sin increased, grace abounded all the more. So that, as sin

reigned in death, grace also might reign through righteousness, leading to eternal life through Jesus Christ our Lord.

Romans 5:7-9 ESV
For one will scarcely die for a righteous person—though perhaps for a good person one would dare even to die— but God shows his love for us in that while we were still sinners, Christ died for us. Since, therefore, we have now been justified by his blood, much more shall we be saved by him from the wrath of God.

Romans 6:14-15 ESV
For sin will have no dominion over you, since you are not under law but under grace. What then? Are we to sin because we are not under law but under grace? By no means!

WAITING ON THE LORD

To wait means to look for, to expect, to stay, or to tarry. David, amid all the conflicts in his life, spoke with confidence. "I remain confident of this: I will see the goodness of the Lord in the land of the living. Wait for the Lord; be strong and take heart and wait for the Lord." The word "confident" means assured, bold, and strong belief. Waiting on the Lord to see His goodness can align with God seeing your obedience or your ability to endure with confidence as you wait. "Though it tarries, wait for it; Because it will surely come, It will not tarry...But the just shall live by his faith."

Galatians 5:5 ESV
For through the Spirit, by faith, we ourselves eagerly wait for the hope of righteousness.

Galatians 6:9 NKJV
And let us not grow weary while doing good, for in due season we shall reap if we do not lose heart.

Isaiah 25:9 KJV
And it shall be said in that day, Lo, this is our God; we have waited for him, and he will save us: this is the Lord; we have waited for him, we will be glad and rejoice in his salvation.

Isaiah 30:18 NIV
Yet the Lord longs to be gracious to you; therefore, he will rise up to show you compassion. For the Lord is a God of justice. Blessed are all who wait for him!

Micah 7:7 ESV
But as for me, I will look to the Lord; I will wait for the God of my salvation; my God will hear me.

Isaiah 33:2 ESV
O Lord, be gracious to us; we wait for you. Be our arm every morning, our salvation in the time of trouble.

Isaiah 49:23 ESV
Kings shall be your foster fathers, and their queens your nursing mothers. With their

faces to the ground, they shall bow down to you, and lick the dust of your feet. Then you will know that I am the Lord; those who wait for me shall not be put to shame.

Isaiah 64:4 KJV
For since the beginning of the world, men have not heard, nor perceived by the ear, neither hath the eye seen, O God, beside thee, what he hath prepared for him that waiteth for him.

James 5:7 AMP
So wait patiently, brothers and sisters, until the coming of the Lord. The farmer waits [expectantly] for the precious harvest from the land, being patient about it, until it receives the early and late rains.

Lamentations 3:26 KJV
It is good that a man should both hope and quietly wait for the salvation of the Lord.

Psalm 62:5 KJV
My soul, wait thou only upon God; for my expectation is from him.

Titus 2:13-14 KJV
Teaching us that, denying ungodliness and worldly lusts, we should live soberly, righteously, and godly, in this present world; Looking for that blessed hope, and the glorious appearing of the great God and our Saviour Jesus Christ.

Lamentations 3:25 NKJV
The Lord is good to those who wait for Him, to the soul who seeks Him.

Psalm 27:14 ESV
Wait for the Lord; be strong, and let your heart take courage; wait for the Lord!

Habakkuk 2:3 ESV
For still the vision awaits its appointed time; it hastens to the end—it will not lie. If it seems slow, wait for it; it will surely come; it will not delay.

Isaiah 40:31 KJV
But they that wait upon the Lord shall renew their strength; they shall mount up with wings as eagles; they shall run, and

not be weary; and they shall walk, and not faint.

Psalm 37:7 ESV
Be still before the Lord and wait patiently for him; fret not yourself over the one who prospers in his way, over the man who carries out evil devices!

I Corinthians 1:4-7 TLB
I can never stop thanking God for all the wonderful gifts he has given you, now that you are Christ's: He has enriched your whole life. He has helped you speak out for him and has given you a full understanding of the truth; what I told you Christ could do for you has happened! Now you have every grace and blessing; every spiritual gift and power for doing his will are yours during this time of waiting for the return of our Lord Jesus Christ.

Proverbs 20:22 ESV
Do not say, "I will repay evil"; wait for the Lord, and he will deliver you.

Psalm 130:5 AMP
I wait [patiently] for the Lord, my soul [expectantly] waits, and in His word do I hope.

Acts 1:4 CEV
While he was still with them, he said: "Don't leave Jerusalem yet. Wait here for the Father to give you the Holy Spirit, just as I told you he has promised to do."

Galatians 5:22-23 AMP
But the fruit of the Spirit [the result of His presence within us] is love [unselfish concern for others], joy, [inner] peace, patience [not the ability to wait, but how we act while waiting], kindness, goodness, faithfulness, gentleness, self-control. Against such things there is no law.

PERSEVERANCE AND ENDURANCE

To persevere is the ability to wait patiently on God, despite any opposition, with a cheerful attitude of confidence, trusting and knowing that His promises to you will not fail. Endurance is the ability or strength to stand despite what comes against you. It is a way of measuring our maturity in Christ. "For you have need of steadfast patience and endurance, so that you may perform and fully accomplish the will of God, and thus receive and carry away [and enjoy to the full] what is promised." Hebrews 10:36 AMP

James 1:12 ESV
Blessed is the man who remains steadfast under trial, for when he has stood the test, he will receive the crown of life, which God has promised to those who love him.

Galatians 6:9 AMP
Let us not grow weary or become discouraged in doing good, for at the

proper time we will reap, if we do not give in.

Hebrews 12:1 ESV
Therefore, since we are surrounded by so great a cloud of witnesses, let us also lay aside every weight, and sin which clings so closely, and let us run with endurance the race that is set before us.

1 Chronicles 16:11 KJV
Seek the Lord and his strength, seek his face continually.

2 Thessalonians 3:13 AMP
And as for [the rest of] you, believers, do not grow tired or lose heart in doing good [but continue doing what is right without weakening].

1 Corinthians 13:7 NLT
Love never gives up, never loses faith, is always hopeful, and endures through every circumstance.

1 Corinthians 15:58 AMP
Therefore, my beloved brothers and sisters, be steadfast, immovable, always excelling in the work of the Lord [always doing your best and doing more than is needed], being continually aware that your labor [even to the point of exhaustion] in the Lord is not futile nor wasted [it is never without purpose].

Hebrews 10:36 NKJV
For you have need of endurance, so that after you have done the will of God, you may receive the promise:

1 Corinthians 16:13 ESV
Be watchful, stand firm in the faith, act like men, be strong.

1 Corinthians 9:24 ESV
Do you not know that in a race all the runners run, but only one receives the prize? So run that you may obtain it.

2 Timothy 2:12 NLB
If we endure hardship, we will reign with him. If we deny him, he will deny us.

2 Thessalonians 1:4 ESV
Therefore, we ourselves boast about you in the churches of God for your steadfastness and faith in all your persecutions and in the afflictions that you are enduring.

Philippians 4:13 KJV
I can do all things through Christ, which strengtheneth me.

Romans 5:3-4 NIV
Not only so, but we also glory in our sufferings, because we know that suffering produces perseverance; perseverance, character; and character, hope.

Matthew 24:11-15 KJV
And many false prophets shall rise, and shall deceive many. And because iniquity shall abound, the love of many shall wax cold. But he that shall endure unto the end, the same shall be saved.

Romans 15:5-6 ESV
May the God of endurance and encouragement grant you to live in such harmony with one another, in accord with Christ Jesus, that together you may with one voice glorify the God and Father of our Lord Jesus Christ.

2 Corinthians 1:6 NLT
Even when we are weighed down with troubles, it is for your comfort and salvation! For when we ourselves are comforted, we will certainly comfort you. Then you can patiently endure the same things we suffer.

Ephesians 6:10-13 KJV
Finally, my brethren, be strong in the Lord, and in the power of his might. Put on the whole armour of God, that ye may be able to stand against the wiles of the devil. For we wrestle not against flesh and blood, but against principalities, against powers, against the rulers of the darkness of this world, against spiritual wickedness in high places. Wherefore take unto you the whole

armour of God, that ye may be able to withstand in the evil day, and having done all, to stand.

FEAR

Fear is a spirit. God has not given us the spirit of fear, but of power, of love, and of a sound mind. When you allow fear in, it does not come alone. It brings with it the spirit of torment. Together, they totally incapacitate you, weakening your power (dunamis-ability), bringing self-centeredness and an inability to think soundly, and undermining self-discipline and self-control. It is a bondage that we cannot afford to take on again, which we have been delivered from by Jesus Christ our Lord. "There is no fear in love. But perfect love drives out fear, because fear has to do with punishment. The one who fears is not made perfect in love." 1 John 4:18 NIV

Psalm 27:1 KJV
The Lord is my light and my salvation; whom shall I fear? The Lord is the strength of my life; of whom shall I be afraid?

Psalm 55:22 AMP
Cast your burden on the Lord [release it] and He will sustain and uphold you; He will

never allow the righteous to be shaken (slip, fall, fail).

Deuteronomy 31:6 NIV
Be strong and courageous. Do not be afraid or terrified because of them, for the Lord your God goes with you; he will never leave you nor forsake you.

Isaiah 41:13 NIV
For I am the Lord your God who takes hold of your right hand and says to you, Do not fear; I will help you.

Psalm 46:1 KJV
God is our refuge and strength, a very present help in trouble.

Psalm 118:6-7 ESV
The Lord is on my side; I will not fear. What can man do to me? The Lord is on my side as my helper; I shall look in triumph on those who hate me.

Proverbs 29:25 NIV
Fear of man will prove to be a snare, but whoever trusts in the Lord is kept safe.

Mark 4:39-40 KJV
And he arose, and rebuked the wind, and said unto the sea, Peace, be still. And the wind ceased, and there was a great calm. And he said unto them, Why are ye so fearful? How is it that ye have no faith?

Psalm 34:7 NIV
The angel of the Lord encamps around those who fear him, and he delivers them.

1 Peter 3:14 NLT
But even if you suffer for doing what is right, God will reward you for it. So don't worry or be afraid of their threats.

Psalm 34:4 KJV
I sought the Lord, and he heard me, and delivered me from all my fears.

Isaiah 41:10 NIV
So do not fear, for I am with you; do

not be dismayed, for I am your God. I will strengthen you and help you; I will uphold you with my righteous right hand.

Psalm 56:3 ESV
When I am afraid, I put my trust in you.

Philippians 4:6-7 NIV
Do not be anxious about anything, but in every situation, by prayer and petition, with thanksgiving, present your requests to God. And the peace of God, which transcends all understanding, will guard your hearts and your minds in Christ Jesus.

John 14:27 KJV
Peace I leave with you, my peace I give unto you: not as the world giveth, give I unto you. Let not your heart be troubled, neither let it be afraid.

2 Timothy 1:7 NKJV
For God has not given us a spirit of fear, but of power and of love and of a sound mind.

1 John 4:18 AMP
There is no fear in love [dread does not exist], but full-grown (complete, perfect) love turns fear out of doors and expels every trace of terror! For fear brings with it the thought of punishment, and [so] he who is afraid has not reached the full maturity of love [is not yet grown into love's complete perfection].

Psalm 94:19 NKJV
In the multitude of my anxieties within me, your comforts delight my soul.

Isaiah 43:1 KJV
But now thus saith the Lord that created thee, O Jacob, and he that formed thee, O Israel, Fear not: for I have redeemed thee, I have called thee by thy name; thou art mine.

Proverbs 12:25 NKJV
Anxiety in the heart of man causes depression, but a good word makes it glad.

Psalm 23:4 ESV
Even though I walk through the valley of the shadow of death, I will fear no evil, for you are with me; your rod and your staff, they comfort me.

Joshua 1:9 AMP
Have I not commanded you? "Be strong and courageous! Do not be terrified or dismayed (intimidated), for the Lord your God is with you wherever you go."

Matthew 6:34 ESV
Therefore, do not be anxious about tomorrow, for tomorrow will be anxious for itself. Sufficient for the day is its own trouble.

1 Peter 5:6-7 NLT
So humble yourselves under the mighty power of God, and at the right time he will lift you up in honor. Give all your worries and cares to God, for he cares about you.

Isaiah 35:4 NKJV
Say to those who are fearful-hearted,

"Be strong, do not fear! Behold, your God will come with vengeance, with the recompense of God; He will come and save you."

Deuteronomy 3:22 KJV
Ye shall not fear them: for the Lord your God he shall fight for you.

Revelation 1:17 NKJV
And when I saw Him, I fell at His feet as dead. But He laid His right hand on me, saying to me, "Do not be afraid; I am the First and the Last. I am He who lives, and was dead, and behold, I am alive forevermore. Amen. And I have the keys of Hades and of Death."

Mark 5:36 NIV
Overhearing what they said, Jesus told him, "Don't be afraid; just believe."

Romans 8:38-39 NIV
For I am convinced that neither death nor life, neither angels nor demons, neither the present nor the future, nor any powers, 39

neither height nor depth, nor anything else in all creation, will be able to separate us from the love of God that is in Christ Jesus our Lord.

Zephaniah 3:17 NKJV
The Lord your God in your midst, The Mighty One, will save; He will rejoice over you with gladness, He will quiet you with His love, He will rejoice over you with singing.

Psalm 91:1-16 NLT
Those who live in the shelter of the Most High will find rest in the shadow of the Almighty. This I declare about the Lord: He alone is my refuge, my place of safety; he is my God, and I trust him. For he will rescue you from every trap and protect you from deadly disease. He will cover you with his feathers. He will shelter you with his wings. His faithful promises are your armor and protection. Do not be afraid of the terrors of the night, nor the arrow that flies in the day. Do not dread the disease that stalks in darkness, nor

the disaster that strikes at midday. Though a thousand fall at your side, though ten thousand are dying around you, these evils will not touch you. Just open your eyes, and see how the wicked are punished. If you make the Lord your refuge, if you make the Most High your shelter, no evil will conquer you; no plague will come near your home. For he will order his angels to protect you wherever you go. They will hold you up with their hands so you won't even hurt your foot on a stone. You will trample upon lions and cobras; you will crush fierce lions and serpents under your feet! The Lord says, "I will rescue those who love me. I will protect those who trust in my name. When they call on me, I will answer. I will be with them in trouble. I will rescue and honor them. I will reward them with a long life and give them my salvation."

A HEART AFTER GOD

David was a man after God's own heart because he was a man of faith who sought after God. He repented quickly when he sinned against Him. He was a man of integrity, even when King Saul tried to kill him. King David was a true worshipper who loved the Lord his God with all his heart! Despite his failures, he knew God's mercy. For man looks at the outward appearance, but God looks at the heart. Does God have first place in your heart?

Philippians 4:6–7 NIV
Do not be anxious about anything, but in every situation, by prayer and petition, with thanksgiving, present your requests to God. And the peace of God, which transcends all understanding, will guard your hearts and your minds in Christ Jesus.

Ephesians 5:2 ESV
And walk in love, as Christ loved us and gave himself up for us, a fragrant offering and sacrifice to God.

Proverbs 23:26 NKJV
My son, give me your heart and let your eyes delight in my ways.

Romans 15:13 NIV
May the God of hope fill you with all joy and peace as you trust in Him, so that you may overflow with hope by the power of the Holy Spirit.

Ephesians 6:6 ESV
Not by the way of eye-service, as people-pleasers, but as servants of Christ, doing the will of God from the heart.

Acts 13:22 ESV
And when he had removed him, he raised up David to be their king, of whom He testified and said, "I have found in David the son of Jesse a man after My heart, who will do all My will."

1 Samuel 13:14 ESV
But now your kingdom shall not continue. The Lord has sought out a man after his own heart, and the Lord has commanded him to be prince over his people, because you have not kept what the Lord commanded you.

1 Samuel 16:7 ESV
But the Lord said to Samuel, "Do not look on his appearance or on the height of his stature, because I have rejected him. For the Lord sees not as man sees: man looks on the outward appearance, but the Lord looks on the heart."

Psalm 51:1-4 ESV
Have mercy on me, O God, according to your steadfast love; according to your abundant mercy blot out my transgressions. Wash me thoroughly from my iniquity, and cleanse me from my sin! For I know my transgressions, and my sin is ever before me. Against you, you only, have I sinned and done

what is evil in your sight, so that you may be justified in your words and blameless in your judgment.

Psalm 42:1-2 NKJV
As the deer pants for the water brooks,
So pants my soul for You, O God. My soul thirsts for God, for the living God.
When shall I come and appear before God?

Proverbs 21:2 ESV
Every way of a man is right in his own eyes, but the Lord weighs the heart.

Romans 12:2 ESV
Do not be conformed to this world, but be transformed by the renewal of your mind, that by testing you may discern what is the will of God, what is good and acceptable and perfect.

1 John 3:22 ESV
And whatever we ask we receive from him, because we keep his commandments and do what pleases him.

Hebrews 13:16 ESV
Do not neglect to do good and to share what you have, for such sacrifices are pleasing to God.

Psalm 147:10-11 ESV
His delight is not in the strength of the horse, nor his pleasure in the legs of a man, but the Lord takes pleasure in those who fear him, in those who hope in his steadfast love.

Psalm 86:10-12 NKJV
For You are great, and do wondrous things; You alone are God. Teach me Your way, O Lord; I will walk in Your truth; Unite my heart to fear Your name. I will praise You, O Lord my God, with all my heart, and I will glorify Your name forevermore.

GOD'S TIMING

The timing of God leaves us at times baffled as we wait on His appearance and hand of deliverance, for restoration, for help. His timing is not like ours, nor is He in an anxious, worried, or concerned state in the manifestation of our prayers. Even with salvation, the timing of His return was set before the foundation was laid. "Nevertheless, do not let this one fact escape you, beloved, that with the Lord one day is as a thousand years and a thousand years as one day. The Lord does not delay and is not tardy or slow about what He promises, according to some people's conception of slowness, but He is long-suffering (extraordinarily patient) toward you, not desiring that any should perish, but that all should turn to repentance" (2 Peter 3:8-9 AMPC). Therefore, He has not forgotten, and neither is He slow in all His promises for you, but patiently waiting and directing you to get in place to receive them.

Habakkuk 2:3 ESV
For still the vision awaits its appointed time; it hastens to the end—it will not lie. If it seems slow, wait for it; it will surely come; it will not delay.

Ecclesiastes 3:1 NKJV
To everything there is a season, A time for every purpose under heaven.

Isaiah 40:31 ESV
But they who wait for the Lord shall renew their strength; they shall mount up with wings like eagles; they shall run and not be weary; they shall walk and not faint.

Psalm 27:14 ESV
Wait for the Lord; be strong, and let your heart take courage; wait for the Lord!

Ecclesiastes 3:11 ESV
He has made everything beautiful in its time. Also, he has put eternity into man's heart, yet so that he cannot find out what God has done from the beginning to the end.

Ecclesiastes 8:6 ESV
For there is a time and a way for everything, although man's trouble lies heavy on him.

Galatians 6:9 ESV
And let us not grow weary of doing good, for in due season we will reap, if we do not give up.

2 Peter 3:8 ESV
But do not overlook this one fact, beloved, that with the Lord one day is as a thousand years, and a thousand years as one day.

Proverbs 3:5-6 ESV
Trust in the Lord with all your heart, and do not lean on your own understanding. In all your ways acknowledge him, and he will make straight your paths.

Lamentations 3:25-26 ESV
The Lord is good to those who wait for him, to the soul who seeks him. It is good that one should wait quietly for the salvation of the Lord.

Acts 1:7 ESV
He said to them, "It is not for you to know times or seasons that the Father has fixed by his own authority.

Psalm 31:15 ESV
My times are in your hand; rescue me from the hand of my enemies and from my persecutors!

Galatians 4:4 ESV
But when the fullness of time had come, God sent forth his Son, born of woman, born under the law.

Romans 8:28 ESV
And we know that for those who love God, all things work together for good, for those who are called according to his purpose.

Luke 18:27 ESV
But he said, "What is impossible with men is possible with God."

Psalm 37:7 ESV
Be still before the Lord and wait patiently for him; fret not yourself over the one who prospers in his way, over the man who carries out evil devices!

Romans 5:6 ESV
For while we were still weak, at the right time Christ died for the ungodly.

Jeremiah 29:11 ESV
For I know the plans I have for you, declares the Lord, plans for welfare and not for evil, to give you a future and a hope.

Micah 7:7 ESV
But as for me, I will look to the Lord; I will wait for the God of my salvation; my God will hear me.

Psalm 46:10 ESV
Be still, and know that I am God. I will be exalted among the nations, I will be exalted in the earth!

Hebrews 6:12 ESV
So that you may not be sluggish, but imitators of those who through faith and patience inherit the promises.

2 Peter 3:8-9 ESV
But do not overlook this one fact, beloved, that with the Lord one day is as a thousand years, and a thousand years as one day. The Lord is not slow to fulfill his promise as some count slowness, but is patient toward you, not wishing that any should perish, but that all should reach repentance.

Isaiah 55:8-9 ESV
For my thoughts are not your thoughts, neither are your ways my ways, declares the Lord. For as the heavens are higher than the earth, so are my ways higher than your ways and my thoughts than your thoughts.

John 7:6 ESV
Jesus said to them, "My time has not yet come, but your time is always here."

2 Corinthians 12:9 ESV
But he said to me, "My grace is sufficient for you, for my power is made perfect in weakness." Therefore, I will boast all the more gladly of my weaknesses, so that the power of Christ may rest upon me.

Ephesians 2:10 ESV
For we are his workmanship, created in Christ Jesus for good works, which God prepared beforehand, that we should walk in them.

Mark 1:15 ESV
And saying, "The time is fulfilled, and the kingdom of God is at hand; repent and believe in the gospel."

Ecclesiastes 3:17 ESV
I said in my heart, God will judge the righteous and the wicked, for there is a time for every matter and for every work.

Psalm 90:4 ESV
For a thousand years in your sight are but as yesterday when it is past, or as a watch in the night.

2 Peter 3:9 ESV
The Lord is not slow to fulfill his promise as some count slowness, but is patient toward you, not wishing that any should perish, but that all should reach repentance.

Psalm 90:12 ESV
So teach us to number our days, that we may get a heart of wisdom.

John 13:7 ESV
Jesus answered him, "What I am doing you do not understand now, but afterward you will understand."

Psalm 37:34 ESV
Wait for the Lord and keep his way, and he will exalt you to inherit the land; you will look on when the wicked are cut off.

Psalm 62:1-2 ESV
For God alone my soul waits in silence; from him comes my salvation. He only is my rock and my salvation, my fortress; I shall not be greatly shaken.

Genesis 21:2 ESV
And Sarah conceived and bore Abraham a son in his old age, at the time of which God had spoken to him.

Psalm 75:2 ESV
At the set time that I appoint, I will judge with equity.

Ephesians 1:10 ESV
As a plan for the fullness of time, to unite all things in him, things in heaven and things on earth.

FAMILY, SINGLES, MARRIAGE, AND CHILDREN

We are the family of the Living God which we were created in His Image and Likeness to walk and live in unity with Him, His Son, and His Spirit. Singleness is a time of living as one in Christ. It's learning who He is and who you are in Him. Marriage is the demonstration of the relationship of Christ to us, His Bride. And children, a demonstration of child-like faith and the attitude that we should possess as we come to the Father.

Matthew 19:4-6 NKJV
And He answered and said to them, "Have you not read that He who made them at the beginning made them male and female, and said, 'For this reason a man shall leave his father and mother and be joined to his wife, and the two shall become one flesh?' So then, they are no longer two but one flesh. Therefore, what God has joined together, let not man separate."

1 Corinthians 11:3 AMPC
But I want you to know *and* realize that Christ is the Head of every man, the head of a woman is her husband, and the Head of Christ is God.

Ephesians 6:1-3 TLB
Children, obey your parents; this is the right thing to do because God has placed them in authority over you. Honor your father and mother. This is the first of God's Ten Commandments that ends with a promise. And this is the promise: that if you honor your father and mother, yours will be a long life, full of blessing.

1 Peter 3:7 AMPC
In the same way you married men should live considerately with [your wives], with an intelligent recognition [of the marriage relation], honoring the woman as [physically] the weaker, but [realizing that you] are joint heirs of the grace (God's unmerited favor) of life, in order that your prayers may not be hindered

and cut off. [Otherwise, you cannot pray effectively].

Proverbs 22:6 NKJV
Train up a child in the way he should go, and when he is old, he will not depart from it.

I Corinthians 7:1-3 AMP
Now as to the matters of which you wrote: It is good (beneficial, advantageous) for a man not to touch a woman [outside marriage]. But because of [the temptation to participate in] sexual immorality, let each man have his own wife, and let each woman have her own husband. The husband must fulfill his [marital] duty to his wife [with good will and kindness], and likewise the wife to her husband.

I Corinthians 7:12-14 ESV
To the rest I say (I, not the Lord) that if any brother has a wife who is an unbeliever, and she consents to live with him, he should not divorce her. If any

woman has a husband who is an unbeliever, and he consents to live with her, she should not divorce him. For the unbelieving husband is made holy because of his wife, and the unbelieving wife is made holy because of her husband. Otherwise, your children would be unclean, but as it is, they are holy.

1 Corinthians 7:3-5 AMPC
The husband should give to his wife her conjugal rights (goodwill, kindness, and what is due her as his wife), and likewise the wife to her husband. For the wife does not have [exclusive] authority and control over her own body, but the husband [has his rights]; likewise also the husband does not have [exclusive] authority and control over his body, but the wife [has her rights]. Do not refuse and deprive and defraud each other [of your due marital rights], except perhaps by mutual consent for a time, so that you may devote yourselves unhindered to prayer. But afterwards resume marital relations, lest Satan tempt you [to sin] through your lack

of restraint of sexual desire.

1 Corinthians 7:8-9 TLB
So I say to those who aren't married and to widows—better to stay unmarried if you can, just as I am. But if you can't control yourselves, go ahead and marry. It is better to marry than to burn with lust.

1 Corinthians 7:34 KJV
There is also a difference also between a wife and a virgin. The unmarried woman careth for the things of the Lord, that she may be holy both in body and in spirit: but she that is married careth for the things of the world, how she may please her husband.

Hebrews 13:4 NKJV
Marriage is honorable among all, and the bed undefiled; but fornicators and adulterers God will judge.

Genesis 1:27-28 NKJV
So God created man in His own image; in the image of God He created him; male

and female He created them. Then God blessed them, and God said to them, "be fruitful and multiply; fill the earth and subdue it; have dominion over the fish of the sea, over the birds of the air, and over every living thing that moves on the earth."

Genesis 2:24 AMPC
Therefore, a man shall leave his father and his mother and shall become united and cleave to his wife, and they shall become one flesh.

Isaiah 54:13 KJV
And all thy children shall be taught of the Lord; and great shall be the peace of thy children.

Isaiah 49:25b AMPC
For I will contend with him who contends with you, and I will give safety to your children and ease them.

Proverbs 11:20-21 ESV
Those of crooked heart are an abomination to the Lord, but those of blameless ways

are his delight. Be assured, an evil person will not go unpunished, but the offspring of the righteous will be delivered.

Proverbs 31:10-31 ESV
(The Woman Who Fears the Lord) An excellent wife who can find? She is far more precious than jewels. The heart of her husband trusts in her, and he will have no lack of gain. Charm is deceitful, and beauty is vain, but a woman who fears the Lord is to be praised. Give her the fruit of her hands, and let her works praise her in the gates.

Psalm 1:1-3 KJV
Blessed is the man that walketh not in the counsel of the ungodly, nor standeth in the way of sinners, nor sitteth in the seat of the scornful. But his delight is in the law of the Lord; and in his law doth he meditate day and night. And he shall be like a tree planted by the rivers of water, that bringeth forth his fruit in his season; his leaf also shall not wither; and whatsoever he doeth shall prosper.

Psalm 127:3-4 KJV

Lo, children are an heritage of the Lord: and the fruit of the womb is his reward. As arrows are in the hand of a mighty man, so are children of the youth.

Proverbs 13:24 AMPC

He who spares his rod [of discipline] hates his son, but he who loves him disciplines diligently and punishes him early.

1 Timothy 5:8 NKJV

But if anyone does not provide for his own, and especially for those of his household, he has denied the faith and is worse than an unbeliever.

Ephesians 6:4 AMP

Fathers, do not provoke your children to anger [do not exasperate them to the point of resentment with demands that are trivial or unreasonable or humiliating or abusive; nor by showing favoritism or indifference to any of them], but bring them up [tenderly, with lovingkindness] in the discipline and instruction of the Lord.

Colossians 3:21 KJV
Fathers, provoke not your children to anger, lest they be discouraged.

Deuteronomy 6:5-9 ESV
You shall love the Lord your God with all your heart and with all your soul and with all your might. And these words that I command you today shall be in your heart. You shall teach them diligently to your children, and shall talk of them when you sit in your house, and when you walk by the way, and when you lie down, and when you rise. You shall bind them as a sign on your hand, and they shall be as frontlets between your eyes. You shall write them on the doorposts of your house and on your gates.

Proverbs 22:15 KJV
Foolishness is bound in the heart of a child, but the rod of correction shall drive it far from him.

Ephesians 5:22-24 TLB
You wives must submit to your husbands' leadership in the same way you submit to the Lord. For a husband is in charge of his wife in the same way Christ is in charge of

his body, the Church. (He gave his very life to take care of it and be its Savior!) So you wives must willingly obey your husbands in everything, just as the Church obeys Christ.

Ephesians 5:25-29 ESV
Husbands, love your wives, as Christ loved the church and gave himself up for her, that he might sanctify her, having cleansed her by the washing of water with the word, so that he might present the church to himself in splendor, without spot or wrinkle or any such thing, that she might be holy and without blemish. In the same way, husbands should love their wives as their own bodies. He who loves his wife loves himself. For no one ever hated his own flesh, but nourishes and cherishes it, just as Christ does the church.

Ephesians 5:33 NKJV
Nevertheless, let each one of you in particular so love his own wife as himself, and let the wife see that she respects her husband.

Deuteronomy 11:18-19 GNT
Remember these commands and cherish them. Tie them on your arms and wear them on your foreheads as a reminder. Teach them to your children. Talk about them when you are at home and when you are away, when you are resting and when you are working.

Genesis 2:18 ESV
Then the Lord God said, "It is not good that the man should be alone; I will make him a helper fit for him."

Psalm 37:25-26 NKJV
I have been young, and now am old; Yet I have not seen the righteous forsaken, nor his descendants begging bread. He is ever merciful and lends, and his descendants are blessed.

Matthew 19:13-15 AMP
Then children were brought to Jesus so that He might place His hands on them [for a blessing] and pray, but the disciples reprimanded them. But He said, "Leave the children alone, and do not forbid them from coming to Me; for the kingdom of heaven belongs to such as these." After

placing His hands on them [for a blessing], He went on from there.

Matthew 19:6 AMP
So they are no longer two, but one flesh. Therefore, what God has joined together, let no one separate."

Mark 10:7-12 NKJV
For this reason a man shall leave his father and mother and be joined to his wife, and the two shall become one flesh; so then they are no longer two, but one flesh. Therefore, what God has joined together, let no man separate." In the house, His disciples also asked Him again about the same matter. So He said to them, "Whoever divorces his wife and marries another commits adultery against her. And if a woman divorces her husband, and marries another, she commits adultery."

SPIRITUAL WARFARE

In Ephesians 6, Paul talks about putting on the whole armor of God that we may be able to stand against the wiles of the devil. Then, there is I Timothy telling us to fight the good fight of faith. Let us not forget II Corinthians, which declares, "For the weapons of our warfare are not carnal, but mighty through God to the pulling down of strongholds." All these scriptures lead one to believe that a war is underway in the unseen, spiritual realm. Experiencing God's power in this realm will ultimately lead us to glory and victory. The scriptures tell us the battle is not ours, but God's. Yet, the victory is ours when we walk in the truth, power, and authority of His Word, standing in our Blood Redeemed position. As soldiers in His army, we are holding up the Blood-stain banner--ready and alert to fight!

FEAR IS THE ENEMY'S GREATEST WEAPON AGAINST US

2 Timothy 1:7 KJV
For God hath not given us the spirit of fear, but of power, and of love, and of a sound mind.

Joshua 1:9 NKJV
Have I not commanded you? Be strong and of good courage; do not be afraid, nor be dismayed, for the Lord your God is with you wherever you go.

2 Corinthians 10:3-5 KJV
For though we walk in the flesh, we do not war after the flesh:(For the weapons of our warfare are not carnal, but mighty through God to the pulling down of strong holds;) Casting down imaginations, and every high thing that exalteth itself against the knowledge of God, and bringing into captivity every thought to the obedience of Christ.

Know the Strategies of the Enemy

2 Corinthians 11:14 NIV
And no wonder, for Satan himself masquerades as an angel of light.

Isaiah 54:17 NKJV
No weapon formed against you shall prosper, and every tongue which rises against you in judgment, You shall condemn. This is the heritage of the servants of the Lord, and their righteousness is from Me," Says the Lord.

James 4:7 KJV
Submit yourselves therefore to God. Resist the devil, and he will flee from you.

Luke 10:19 AMP
Listen carefully: I have given you authority [that you now possess] to tread on serpents and scorpions, and [the ability to exercise authority] over all the power of the enemy (Satan); and nothing will [in any way] harm you.

1 Peter 5:8 AMP
Be sober [well balanced and self-disciplined], be alert and cautious at all times. That enemy of yours, the devil, prowls around like a roaring lion [fiercely hungry], seeking someone to devour.

1 Thessalonians 5:6 KJV
Therefore, let us not sleep, as do others; but let us watch and be sober.

Romans 8:37 NKJV
No, in all these things we are more than conquerors through him who loved us.

1 John 5:4-5 AMP
For everyone born of God is victorious and overcomes the world; and this is the victory that has conquered and overcome the world—our [continuing, persistent] faith [in Jesus the Son of God]. Who is the one who is victorious and overcomes the world? It is the one who believes and recognizes the fact that Jesus is the Son of God.

Matthew 18:18-20 AMP
I assure you and most solemnly say to you, whatever you bind [forbid, declare to be improper and unlawful] on earth shall have [already] been bound in heaven, and whatever you loose [permit, declare lawful] on earth shall have [already] been loosed in heaven. "Again I say to you, that if two [c]believers on earth agree [that is, are of one mind, in harmony] about

anything that they ask [within the will of God], it will be done for them by My Father in heaven. For where two or three are gathered in My name [meeting together as My followers], I am there among them."

Deuteronomy 28:7 NKJV
The Lord will cause your enemies who rise against you to be defeated before your face; they shall come out against you one way and flee before you seven ways.

Ephesians 6:10-18 NKJV
Finally, my brethren, be strong in the Lord and in the power of His might. Put on the whole armor of God, that you may be able to stand against the wiles of the devil. For we do not wrestle against flesh and blood, but against principalities, against powers, against the rulers of the darkness of this age, against spiritual hosts of wickedness in the heavenly places. Therefore, take up the whole armor of God, that you may be able to withstand in the evil day, and having done all, to stand. Stand therefore, having girded your waist with truth, having put on the breastplate of righteousness, and having shod your feet with the preparation of the gospel of peace; above

all, taking the shield of faith with which you will be able to quench all the fiery darts of the wicked one. And take the helmet of salvation, and the sword of the Spirit, which is the word of God; praying always with all prayer and supplication in the Spirit, being watchful to this end with all perseverance and supplication for all the saints.

Mark 16:15-18 KJV

And he said unto them, Go ye into all the world, and preach the gospel to every creature. He that believeth and is baptized shall be saved; but he that believeth not shall be damned. And these signs shall follow them that believe; In my name shall they cast out devils; they shall speak with new tongues; They shall take up serpents; and if they drink any deadly thing, it shall not hurt them; they shall lay hands on the sick, and they shall recover.

Psalm 84:11 KJV

For the Lord God is a sun and shield: the Lord will give grace and glory: no good thing will he withhold from them that walk uprightly.

Psalm 121:5-8 TLB
Jehovah himself is caring for you! He is your defender. He protects you day and night. He keeps you from all evil and preserves your life. He keeps his eye upon you as you come and go, and always guards you.

2 Timothy 2:4 KJV
No man that warreth entangleth himself with the affairs of this life; that he may please him who hath chosen him to be a soldier.

Romans 8:31 KJV
What shall we then say to these things? If God be for us, who can be against us?

To be continued

Sources

https://biblereasons.com/distractions

Quotespedia.org

https://www.biblegateway.com/

ABOUT THE AUTHOR

Anita Williams is an Associate Pastor and a retired Educator, who believes that knowledge is power. She stands on and adheres to the scripture out of Hosea 4:6a, "My people are destroyed for lack of knowledge [of My law, where I reveal My will]." She believes that knowing and abiding in the Word of God is an advantage and benefit for living a strong and successful Christian life. She believes when you pray the word of God, Heaven opens up, and God bows down to open His ear in attentiveness because you find delight in His Word. As we take in the Word daily, it's like Him giving us our daily bread. *"Your words were found, and I ate them. 'And Your words became for me a joy and the delight of my heart; For I have been called by Your name, O Lord God of hosts."* Jeremiah 15:16

Anita is a devoted mother of eight beautiful, spirit-filled children (including her children's spouses), a grandmother, and a great-grandmother. As an educator, she served as a teacher and an Administrator. As an Associate Pastor, her duties have included "Education and Spiritual Development" and, later, serving as the department head for "Communication" and "Intercession". Once, an entrepreneur, co-owner of "Rhema", a company that tutors elementary through high school students, and also the co-founder of the ministry, Anointed by Christ (a ministry of prayer). Our vision is to see women strengthened and grow spiritually as they discover their God-given gifts, enabling them to walk into their God-ordained purpose. We desire to usher women into the newness of life in Christ Jesus. In addition to her educational qualifications, she holds a Master's in Business Administration and a Doctorate in Christian Theology. Ms. Williams has spoken at workshops, retreats, and conferences to both youth and adults.

Anita's deepest desire is for the Body of Christ to know that God's divine power has given us all things that pertain to life and godliness, in His Word and through His Holy Spirit. "His Word does not return to Him void, but it shall accomplish that which He purposes, and shall succeed in the thing for which He sent it." So, know that His Word is TRUTH, and in His Word you shall know the truth, and the truth shall make you free! His Way is His Will, and His Will is found in His Word.

"*Now this is the confidence that we have in Him, that if we ask anything according to His will, He hears us. And if we know that He hears us, whatever we ask, we know that we have the petitions that we have asked of Him."* I John 5:14-15

www.ingramcontent.com/pod-product-compliance
Lightning Source LLC
LaVergne TN
LVHW050622100826
845148LV00011B/1696

* 9 7 9 8 2 3 4 0 0 2 4 2 6 *